# UNLEARNING
# THE LIE

## Sexism in School

# UNLEARNING THE LIE

## Sexism in School

Barbara Grizzuti Harrison

William Morrow & Company, Inc.
New York   1974

Library of Congress Catalog Card Number 73-16209

ISBN 0-688-05236-3 (pbk.)

**Library of Congress Cataloging in Publication Data**

Harrison, Barbara Grizzuti.
  Unlearning the lie.

  Bibliography: p.
  1. Sex instruction. 2. Sex role. 3. Woman—Psychology. I. Title.
HQ57.5.A3H37 1974  301.41'07  73-16209
ISBN 0-688-05236-3 (pbk.)

*This book is for Anna and Josh*

Probably all education is but two
things, first, parrying of the ignorant
children's impetuous assault on the
truth and, second, gentle, imperceptible
initiation of the humiliated children
into the lie.

—FRANZ KAFKA

# Contents

*Preface*        *ix*

Introduction: Boys Will Be Boys/Girls Will Be Girls    *1*

1. Woodward: Why Change a Good Thing?    *12*
2. Summer 1970: A Beginning    *26*
3. Fall and Winter 1970: Politicizing Feelings    *43*
4. Winter 1970: Changes    *60*
5. Consciousness-raising or Political Activity?    *68*
6. Black and White    *78*
7. Men and Women    *113*
8. June 1971: A New Beginning    *131*
9. Changes, 1971–1972    *161*

*Bibliography*        *175*

# Preface

Almost a hundred years ago, radical educator Maria Montessori said, "To serve the children is to feel one is serving the spirit of man." Now, a century later, women are beginning to understand that this prophetic female was right, though in a way that she surely did not intend. Modern education is indeed serving the needs and the spirit of Man, but it is leaving Woman outside in a cold and lonely place, a sterile place from which she cannot apprehend her past or grasp her own future, a shadowy, mirrored isolation-booth from which she perceives her present, her nature, and her needs only as reflections of the necessities of Man.

It took centuries to bend Adam's rib into the shape of a walking, talking Barbie Doll; it took an elaborate system of rewards and punishments to convince Woman that she was Womb. But many of us experience feminism as a religious conversion—a leap into belief. Suddenly a whole lot that was cloudy becomes very clear. The force of the magic wears off, of course; and what one is left with is not a mystery solved entire but a determination no longer to be a complicitor in one's own victimization: a need to invent a self.

From the first recognition that—as women—we have no past, no history, no religion of our own, that we are in fact given over to the necessities of others, we proceed to the difficult task of reconstruction. We form our own past (or our own version of it, which comes to the same thing), we will our own necessities (escaping the prison of definitions imposed upon us by others), we create our own natures, we determine our own needs. The will to create a self, to give birth to a past, a present, and a future not delivered to us by Man, takes varied forms. For some women it means writing the poem they never before found time to write, or discovering the female poet whose voice is their own; for some it means fighting legal battles in courts; for some it means discovering the will to love a once-hated mother whose fate they feared would be theirs; for some it means a restructuring of their marriage; for some it is as simple as finding the voice to say *I hate housework and refuse to carry the burden of it alone*. For others it means choosing a work in the world that is truly their own, or a newfound ability to say *Yes* or *No* to man or state, child or boss, construction worker, lover, or mate, in accordance with the imperatives of their own natures, in voices that no longer sound faint.

For perhaps a score of feminists I know well, it meant taking an enlightened look at the education of their daughters and of their sons, recognizing that it had, in large measure, failed them, and seeking to redress that wrong.

This book is an account of our struggle to provide for our girls and our boys an alternative to sexist education, an education that will serve not merely the spirit of man but the spirit and needs of individual women as well; an education that is truly free because it is truly human and not solely male; an education that will allow our children to make their own choices, not limit them to choices based on gender.

What we wanted was visionary, and what we attempted was revolutionary; it was certainly hard and often frustrating work. It is not yet completed. But we made a good beginning.

The place where this happened is The Woodward School, a private, interracial, nonsectarian parent-teacher cooperative in Brooklyn, where our boys and girls attend kindergarten to eighth grade in an atmosphere we were pleased to describe as libertarian and "free."

We were not the first to learn that the hardest question of all to answer is "What do you want?" nor were we the first to understand that the end is often revealed through the means; we learned as we went along. We hope others will take courage from our successes and profit from our mistakes.

Change, and the dynamics of change, are not easy to document. Really this book is not just about curriculum changes, or even about evolving social awarenesses and new teaching methods, or new ways of teachers' relating to boys and to girls (though it is about all of these things too); it is about the way one institution reacted to the demand for change; the way black women and white women worked together, or pulled apart; the way feminist women interacted with feminist men; and it is about tensions and conflicts between parents and professional staff. It is about the way women and men of goodwill—and their children—wrestled with that angel, change.

In the course of writing this book, I interviewed men and women, parents, and staff members who were involved in the struggle for nonsexist education at Woodward. I am grateful to them for their political and psychological insights. No one, of course, experiences the same events in the same way, so, while I do very much hope that this book will serve as a blueprint for other feminists who are concerned to provide a nonsexist education for their daughters and sons, the interpretation of events is, necessarily, mine. I hope that it will reflect as fully as possible the reality of the feminists I am thankful to have worked with. We all hope that others—for love of their daughters, and in the tender hope that their sons will be free from the blinding necessity to dominate and secure their right to rule, and with the conviction that neither their boys nor their girls must be victims or victimizers—will make a beginning.

I must acknowledge my indebtedness to all the members of the Sex-roles Committee of Woodward, to the Black Studies Committee, and to Woodward's staff. In particular, I wish to thank Hirsch Grunstein, Bart Meyers, Bob Ubell; and Mimi Anderson, Terry Babb, Donna Barkman, Meg Bluhm, Cora Lynne David, Ruth Fishman, Gertrude Goldstein, Marge Hammock, Trudy Lamb, Francine Lerner, Carol London, Barbara Mask, Peggy Sandback, Maia Scherrer, Vivian Ubell, Brett Vuolo, and Adrienne Yurick, who helped lay to rest the mischievous lie that women are incapable of generous friendship.

I need especially to thank Andrea Ostrum. I am chagrined to remember how, when Andrea first publicly raised the issue of sex-role discrimination at a parent-teacher meeting at Woodward in

1970, I slid down in my seat, embarrassed and ashamed that a member of my sex was calling attention to herself and to all of us over what then seemed to me a frivolous and inconsequential matter. I like to think that what has happened since then is not so much that I have learned to take myself seriously (contrary to popular opinion, feminists do laugh at themselves, and laughter, in general among us, is not an exceptional thing), but that I have learned that *femaleness* is not to be despised, that none of us has to apologize for demanding recognition of our rights because none of us has to feel guilty for having been born a woman; I have learned, in fact, that women are human, and that being human they have a right to say *I want.*

This is, properly speaking, a postscript. But my intensity of feeling obliges me to place it here. There is no drama without conflict. And while it is true that there was conflict at Woodward, I hope I haven't fallen into the trap of writing as if the antagonists were "goodies" and "badies." I write from the perspective of a Sex-roles Committee member; but I love individual members of the staff very much. I would not be happy were I not to emphasize my belief that the quarrels we had in no way reflect upon their conscientiousness, honor, and goodness. Woodward is a good place; it is because it is a good place that parents tend, sometimes bitterly, to reproach it when it fails to be perfect. Unhappily, people tend also, with disturbing frequency, to see teachers as servants of the will of parents. Teachers are not our servants—any more than parents and teachers are servants of the children they guide and protect. If—whether out of feminist zeal or a proclivity to see things in terms of absolutes (Right or Wrong)—my writing has smacked, even a little, of that kind of obscene condescension, it is a grave and unwarrantable error.

Writing this book has forced me to reexamine some of my own basic assumptions—I have understood from writing it how much serious hard work is ahead of me; I mean the work of developing an empathetic response to people whose struggles are different from my own, and I mean the work of perceiving clearly the relationship between the personal and the political. My confusions will be evident. I hope they will not be too obtrusive. Where they are obtrusive, I apologize for allowing my "growing pains" to be part of this narrative; and I thank my friends—they will know who they are—who have disturbed my equilibrium, caused me to doubt, and helped me to grow. My gratitude belongs to them; the confusions are no one's fault but my own.

# UNLEARNING
# THE LIE

## Sexism in School

# Introduction

## Boys Will Be Boys/Girls Will Be Girls

Sugar and spice and everything nice,
That's what little girls are made of.
Frogs and snails and puppy dog tails,
That's what little boys are made of.

Freedom does not alter the innate
predilected of the sexes.

—A. S. NEIL

A little girl is treated and molded
differently from a little boy from the
day she is born.

—BENJAMIN SPOCK

To offer the complexities of life as an excuse for not addressing oneself to the simpler, more manageable (trivial) aspects of daily existence is a perversity often indulged in by artists, husbands, intellectuals—and critics of the women's Movement. When feminists focus their attention on the liberation of their children from sex-role stereotypes they often begin at the beginning; they begin, that is, with blocks and dolls. And immediately they are accused of busying themselves unproductively with trivia. (The same charge, however, is seldom leveled against radical therapists whose patients begin at the beginning by re-enacting their blocks-and-dolls childhood.) Feminists are loftily called upon to justify their concern with blocks and dolls; they might just as well be asked to justify Freud's dictum that what

happens in the nursery asserts itself in the man. People whose
lives are messy and confused, painful and unmanageably complex—and who hope that their children's lives will be better, will
be golden and joyous and filled with clarity and delight—often
disdain talk of blocks and dolls. . . . *Trivia!* But they are wrong.
Novelist Joan Didion was wrong when, in her important essay on
the women's Movement, she pointed to feminists' concern with "a
nursery school where the little girls huddled in a 'doll corner' and
were forcibly restrained from playing with building blocks" as
evidence that the basic philosophy of feminism had been trivi-
alized. Didion spoke for many when she questioned what blocks
and dolls have to do with the "irreconcilable difference" of being
a woman, "that sense of living one's deepest life underwater, that
dark involvement with blood and birth and death." But dolls and
blocks do have a great deal to do with that sense of *otherness*,
with the "irreconcilable difference" of being a woman. Revolt
and adventure are not paths open to girls; women sense that men
have a direct and purposeful connection with the world, while
they exist only in connection with men. Keeping girls in the doll
corner, while boys are zipping around, moving, thrusting, making splashy changes in their environment, molding their world,
helps to foster an *artificial* difference, a difference which is perceived, by women, as a lack, and called, by men, "inferiority."
(Perhaps there are *innate* irreconcilable differences other than
the obvious biological ones. But how, huddled in our separate
corner, with no psychic room to exercise free choice, are we to
know that is so?) Girls spend all their young lives playing with
dolls, obsessed with domestic relations; and they grow up needy
and wanting and waiting (for a man), obsessed, to the point of
madness, with their relationships with their men and their children. It is thrilling to read about the obsessions and the madness,
but it is terrible to live with the obsessions and the madness.
Some of us celebrate our pain in poetry; it falls to others to do
something about the culture that produced the madness. No one
wishes to deny the blood and birth and death that are part of our
lives; but most of us, while living our "deepest lives underwater,"
have occasionally to come up for air—to go to the supermarket,
or the orthodontist, or to pick the kids up from their (sexist)
schools. (Even poets take time off from their magical lives to go

to the laundry—unless, of course, their wives do it for them). Nobody claims that by rearranging blocks and dolls feminists hope to create a stark new political-poster world in which ironies and moral ambiguities will not exist. What we say is that we will, hopefully, give our boys and our girls a better way to deal with moral ambiguities, ironies, and despair, by not cruelly limiting the ways they may choose to deal with them.

So, to begin at the (not so trivial) beginning, with blocks and dolls, sugar and spice, snails and puppy dog tails:

In Gesell and Ilg's classic behavioral guide, *The Child from Five to Ten*, there is a rather remarkable sentence: "At two and a half years of age," these experts state, "boys may prefer girls' toys." But, one might reasonably ask, if boys are naturally drawn at an early age to dolls, dollhouses, and housekeeping equipment, what justification exists for calling them *girls'* toys? Gesell and Ilg provide the answer: "The child is taught by suggestion and indirection."

What the child is taught, in fact, is that girls will be (and damn well better be) girls, and that boys will be (and damn well better be) boys. They have to be *carefully* taught; if they are not, say Gesell and Ilg somewhat skittishly, "something unexpected is likely to occur."

As long as we respected the advice of gurus like Dr. Spock, there was small chance that "something unexpected" would occur:

If I had a daughter, I'd dress her in clothes that were different from boys'. If she asked to wear blue jeans like her brother, I'd tell her how much I like to see her looking nice in girls' clothes. When I found her fighting with her brother over a truck that I knew she never paid any attention to when he was away, I'd remind her firmly that she has much more fun with her girls' playthings. Because young girls have a readiness to believe unconsciously that their mothers have not endowed them as well as boys, they need lots of evidence that their mothers enjoy them just because they are girls, just because they can shop together, talk about babies, clothes and interior decoration.

While the belief that they are inadequately endowed may be unconscious, the programming for that belief is overt, if not calculated. To the question, "Why don't I have a penis like Johnnie?" many of us have considered "Girls don't have penises" an appropriate response. Suppose we had said, "You have a womb, breasts, and a clitoris, and Johnnie doesn't"? Would our daughters then have felt underendowed? (It's interesting, by the way, that Spock chooses to project blame on the *mother* for what's supposedly missing from girls. It would be even more interesting to know if he also assigns her the credit for the superior endowment of boys.)

These are the toys Spock exhorted parents to buy for boys: cars, trucks, buses, trains ("partly because they are symbols of masculinity, and also because of the variety of ways and levels in which they can be used"), model cars, planes, trains, boats (because they develop, "not only manual skill, interest in mechanics, and a sense of history, but also basic creativity"), woodworking tools, building sets, and construction sets.

These, he said, must be girls' playthings: dolls, dolls' clothes and equipment, housekeeping equipment, dolls' cribs, prams, bureaus, china and cutlery; child-sized stoves, refrigerators, dining tables, laundry equipment; needlework sets, and bead-stringing sets. These goodies, he said, would inspire girls to "play out . . . dramas of parent-child relationships, friendships, school life, adventure, romance, domestic existence." (In all fairness, he does list one androgynous plaything: a bicycle.)

Dr. Spock claims to have changed his thinking since 1955, when he pooh-poohed "the women called feminists, who are resentful of men's advantages." If he has, the producers of television commercials have not. Trucks are invariably advertised as "boys' toys" (as are war toys, or anything that smacks of dominance or aggression); and you don't catch a boy on the television saying "Look, ma! she walks, she talks, she cries, she wets!"

One wonders about the little boy who, perversely, after the two-and-a-half-year-old magic cut-off time, still wants to play with a doll. "Conscious of the excessive cultural pressure exerted by the disapproval of his parents," say Gesell and Ilg, he believes he is "not orthodox; so he keeps his doll somewhat out of sight." A Woodward feminist reported that a small boy once went to the pathetic extreme of fashioning a stuffed airplane to take to bed to "cuddle," thus, presumably, preserving his orthodox masculine image while satisfying his need to nurture and to gentle.

And what of the little girl who learns—earlier than boys do, according to Gesell and Ilg—her "assigned sex role" (a role which, according to these theorists, "is progressing toward marriage")? If she is not entirely pleased with her vast array of Lilliputian domestic playthings, she might do what one Woodward child was observed to do—push her carriage around with a dump truck in it. That *is* unorthodox.

We are told, by the psychologists who insist on innate temperamental differences between boys and girls—the very same psychologists who dictate what toys boys must have and what toys girls must have) that a three-year-old boy, asked "Are you a little boy or a little girl?" is likely to respond, "No, I am a *big* boy." A three-year-old girl asked the same question is likely to reply, "I'm a boy." Well, no wonder. While a boy is "developing manual skill, an interest in mechanics, a sense of history, and basic creativity," a girl is playing with tiny tea cups. Tiny tea cups pall.

And why, after all, can't a boy "play out . . . dramas of parent-child relationships, friendships, school life, adventure, romance, domestic existence"? Why, indeed! What are we doing to our children?

We are destroying their spontaneity—and therefore, in large part, their joy. We are telling them, "by suggestion and indirection" what is good for them. We are—with benevolent intent but malevolent consequences—assigning them roles based on gender without regard to their individual natures and their needs.

Having done this scrupulously from the moment of their birth (just think how you would have reacted if your baby boy had been wrapped in a pink blanket), we then pronounce, as if it were God's own truth, *Boys will be Boys, Girls will be Girls.* Or, if we are psychologists or educators, we dress up the bromide to sound really heavy and authentic:

"It's a great mistake to try to minimize [temperamental differences] in any way." (Spock)

"To what extent the manifold differences are due to a cultural bias the statistics do not disclose. The bias itself must have been originally produced by innate differences in the sexes. In any

event, the end result is that each sex tends to play the role
assigned to it." (Gesell and Ilg)

"Freedom does not alter the innate predilection of the sexes."
(A. S. Neil)

No parent sets out to be wicked. The man I saw at the zoo
cafeteria who told his little boy to "sit in the blue chair because
you're a boy" probably didn't even hear himself say it (although,
as a matter of fact, he said it three times, and one wonders whose
masculinity was being insisted upon, and how many "symbols of
masculinity" are necessary before a boy can assert his "innate
temperamental difference"). If a feminist had told this father
that what he was doing was part of a whole network of messages
perceived and assimilated by his child that would have consequences in the way the boy would one day understand and act in
the world (not to mention in bed, in his work, with his mother,
with other women, with lovers, and with men), he would have
thought her mad. Yet the messages are daily and unremitting.
They are trivial, perhaps, in each instance, but taken cumula-
tively, they articulate a world-view; they tell our children what it
is to be a male human being, and what it is to be a female human
being.

So it is not carping, and it is not a preoccupation with trivia, to
ask if we are not programming our children from the time they
are given to us to guide and protect, in ways that are designed to
limit and contain them in the straitjacket of gender-based
roles. "Little" things can have big repercussions, as Spock *et al.*
foresaw when they implored us to slap a little girl's wrist if she
presumed to play with symbols of masculinity.

For example:

*A fire engine rushes past your house. Whom do you call to see
it? Your daughter, or your son?*

*You drive past a wedding party. Whose attention do you call to
it? Your son's, or your daughter's?*

*You are given flowers. Whom do you ask to arrange them
prettily in a vase? Your son, or your daughter?*

*Out walking with your children, you pass a woman with a
small baby. With whom do you share your pleasure in the infant?
Your son, or your daughter?*

*A building is under construction. To whom do you point out the crane, the workers, the details of construction? Your daughter or your son?*

*Relatives come to visit. Do they hug and kiss your daughter and tell her how pretty she looks? Do they shake hands with your son, toss him up in the air, and jocularly mess up his hair? Why?*

*Your small son asks for a doll, a toy oven, or a jump rope. How do you react?*

*Your daughter and your son both ask for trucks for Christmas. Who gets the 29¢ truck in the Christmas stocking? Who gets the $9.95 truck under the tree?*

*Would a stranger be able to tell the sex of each of your children from their respective Christmas lists?*

(I gave my daughter a dollhouse this past Christmas; it was what her heart desired. My son's heart desired a football, binoculars, and a pedometer. Like many feminists I know, I am not unwilling to give my children "stereotypical" toys when they are expressly wished for. I see the charm and the magic of a dollhouse—a manageable world—myself. I would reproach myself, however, if all of Anna's toys were "feminine," and if, on the other hand, Josh got all the active-adventure-doing stuff. . . . When Josh—who is ten—was four, he very much admired a girl-playmate's dollhouse—though he confided to me his intention of hiding any dollhouse under his bed that he might be lucky enough to get. I didn't ever give him one—and now I can't think of a single reason, aside from unreasonable fear and prejudice, why I did not. . . . I think it's important to see children in a continuum. Last year, for example, Anna—who is nine—wanted science kits and a camera; she scorned dolls as much as she now takes pleasure in dollhouses. . . . What I'm suggesting is not that parents issue a hammer to a kid who wants a teddy bear, or a Raggedy Ann to a kid who wants a baseball mitt, but that—*from the earliest age*—we expose all our children to the widest possible variety of playthings, and that we begin to look at many more playthings as androgynous and appropriate to either sex.)

*Look at your children's books. In how many is the main character (animal or human) male? In how many is the main character female?*

*Would you be inclined to give your son a book in which the leading personality was a girl? How many books does your daughter have in which the leading personality is a boy?*

*How often have you heard parents say: Boys don't cry. Girls shouldn't fight. Be a man, son. Be a lady, honey. Boys will be boys. Girls will be girls.*

*Your daughter is called a tomboy. Your son is called a sissy. How, in each case, do you react? To which description do you react more negatively? Have you thought about why?*

("Sissy," I think, would undoubtedly scare the hell out of most parents, while "tomboy" would do little more than produce a tolerant smile; and for the same reasons that parents are much more inclined to be fearful of their boys becoming homosexual than their girls. We unconsciously seem to value maleness so much more than we do femaleness: to be a tomboy is, one might say, to be upwardly mobile, while to be a sissy is to ape a despised sex. Considering that men implore women to be "feminine," but jeer at them for being female, it's not surprising that a "feminine" male is very bad news. I think also, that we assume girls will "grow out" of tomboyishness—there is evidence that girls "settle down" to their assigned roles earlier than boys do; trained to be docile and dependent, they know it's in their best survival interests to do so—we make no such assumptions about "sissies." Perhaps the explanation is even simpler: we just never take girls—or their sexuality—seriously.)

And the result: while "four- and five-year-old children often play the role of the opposite sex, . . . by the age of seven, the shifting in roles becomes less frequent." In other words, by the time they're seven, they know what's "orthodox," they know what's good for them, they know what's culturally sanctioned, and they know that their choices are limited by their gender. By "playing the role of the opposite sex," one is not to understand Gesell and Ilg to mean anything as titillating as precocious sexual play. What they mean is "many a four-year-old boy has asked for a doll for Christmas." Why that should be *opposite* to his sex, in view of the fact that Gesell and Ilg themselves say it is *normal*, is not quite clear. They admit that most four-year-olds behave like this, yet they say that such behavior is inappropriate to their sex. The mind boggles.

All of us, children and adults, parents and educators, have learned our lessons well. So well that by the time our rigorously groomed children reach school, this is what we are likely to find, and what feminists at The Woodward School found. In fairness, I must add that some or all staff members will dispute that some of these incidents happened exactly as I have described them. Woodward feminists, however, do almost unanimously perceive them as having happened this way. (As I relate in a later chapter, the telling of "sexist anecdotes" often created contention and conflict, with the staff insisting that our harping on incidents that were "isolated" and "atypical" was unfair and detrimental.) However, even supposing that the stories were exaggerated or distorted in the retelling, no one will believe that they *could not* have happened, because incidents like—and worse than—these happen all the time in all schools.

*Teachers expectations of girls are different from their expectations of boys:* A number of kindergarten children are working at a carpentry bench. A girl shows her teacher (male) her handiwork. "These nails aren't hammered in far enough," he says, "I'll do it for you." A boy shows the teacher his handiwork. "These nails aren't hammered in far enough," the teacher says. "Take the hammer and pound them in all the way."

*The Cinderella Syndrome* (dialogue in a second-grade classroom), six-year-old Mary to student teacher: "Johnnie hates me." Student teacher: "Of course he doesn't hate you. How could anybody hate such a sweet, pretty girl?" Mary: "Oh, yes, he hates me. Ask him." Student teacher to John: "You don't hate Mary, do you?" John: "Yeah, I hate her." Student teacher: "How could you hate anybody so pretty?"

*Boys are expected to be physically aggressive:* A sixth-grade class trip to an ice-skating rink; a boy pushes and shoves a girl, who, falling, retaliates by calling him a four-letter word. A concessionaire who has witnessed the incident later refuses to serve the girl, because "ladies don't talk like that." The girl, irate, complains to the school's director; the director, sympathetic to the girl's feeling of having been messed over, nevertheless counsels her to have "a decent respect for the opinions of others," and suggests that the sensibilities of a hot-dog vendor who is appalled by a girl's using street language have got to be taken into consideration. Somehow the initial provocation—the boy's physical aggression—is overlooked in the discussion of the girl's verbal response.

*Styles differ according to sex:* Boys erect massive block structures; girls tend to build nesty, small-scale constructions. A nursery-school teacher takes a radio apart. The boys rush over, clamoring to see how it works, while the girls, happily festooning one another with the laces and cast-off jewelry of the costume box, stay put. Boys are mobilized by the opportunity of seeing how things function. Girls seem content to engage in passive, ornamental activities.

*Girls relate to aesthetics; boys relate to scientific principles:* A group of first- and second-grade childen is in the playground, observing clouds. The boys discuss the movement of the clouds, the wind, the power that pushes them across the sky. The girls say, "Oooh, aren't they pretty?"

*Sex-role stereotyping is unquestioned:* Eighth-graders discuss *The Grapes of Wrath.* A young girl, asked to define the qualities of Steinbeck's characters, says, "Rose of Sharon is completely obsessed with her pregnancy. That's what she's about." "Ma," says a boy, "gets it all together. The family couldn't make it without her." "Apple-pie mother," interjects another boy, with a laugh that is rather sly. "No, not really," corrects the teacher. "Steinbeck sees woman as earthmother, as a pillar of strength, nurturing, supportive. . . ." "Right! Apple-pie mother," says one of the girls.

*When boys violate girls' physical integrity, the girls are held equally to blame:* Embarrassed third-grade girls complain of boys "pinching their bottoms" and of boys peering over lavatory walls to "spy on them." The teacher suggests to the girls that they were "teasing" the boys, and to the parents that the girls were being "provocative." A parent questions her girl: "Mommy, I was teasing, I guess. But I don't know what I *did*. I don't know *how* I teased. I never touched *them*." *When girls are assaulted, they feel guilty.*

Incidents like these are the stuff education is made of. And the programming and the attitudes that give rise to incidents like these are also reflected in a school's curriculum, in a version of history that centers—literally—around *man's* development, in textbooks, in readers, and in physical activities. Our children are not learning to be their best selves; they are learning what society—male-dominated society—requires females to be, and what society requires males to be.

How do we change the pattern? How do we unlearn the lie that girls are innately passive, unaggressive, supportive, and domestic; that their nature is to need, and to want, and to wait, while boys are innately dominant, achieving, adventurous, and aggressive, their nature to seek and to dominate? How do we free our children to choose their own styles, their own lives, their own pleasures, and their own work? How can we reverse sexist indoctrination so that powerful people of *either* sex may exercise their right to power without having to dissemble, manipulate, pretend, destroy others or themselves in the process? How can we make it possible for nurturing, compassionate people of *either* sex to delight in their own natures without fear of scorn? What is required to make our children fully human, fully aware of all the options available to them? How do we free them to avail themselves of the human privilege of taking their own risks in their own time, and in accordance with their own singular natures regardless of gender?

At the beginning of the 1970–1971 school year, feminists at The Woodward School in Brooklyn formed a "Sex-roles Committee" to explore ways in which Woodward might be perpetuating mind- and spirit-debilitating stereotypical sex roles; their purpose was to help their children unlearn the sexist lie; and this is their story.

# 1

# Woodward: Why Change a Good Thing?

What's good for the goose is good for the gander.

Most education is joyless. I remember my own elementary-school days as one long blur of misery. I was "good," and smart, docile, and obedient—and I was never not frightened. I had a stomachache that lasted from mid-September to late June. I was always afraid of falling out of favor with my teachers, who seemed to me the absolute arbiters of my fate. I was equally afraid of being judged guilty of currying favor with those teachers, knowing that a smartypants teacher's pet was begging trouble from her classmates in exact proportion to the favors she enjoyed from her masters. Consequently—from the day when, in third grade, I brazenly announced that I knew how to spell *postpone* (and was beamed on by Miss Silver and thereafter ignored at games and frowned on by every boy and girl in the class), to the day when I entered Junior High School—I was as self-effacing as it was possible to be without earning the reputation of "dumbie." Maintaining a difficult balance, I learned to suffer in silence.

My younger brother, on the other hand, was—in more ways than one—a big noise. He never suffered, or indeed did anything else, silently. He never felt obliged to study or to do his homework—that was "sissy." He rarely, in fact, felt obliged to go to school at all. He liked to play stickball and to work with his hands; and he refused to see what learning to spell had to do with any of the things he liked or was good at. He was not afraid to say so, and, consequently, on those rare occasions when he did present himself at P.S.41, more often than not he spent his days in the Assistant Principal's office (surrounded, he told me not very tolerantly, by beaverboard gold-starred spelling lists produced by "nice girls" like me), being exhorted to be good and smart and docile and obedient by a woman who informed him that Boys, in any case, would be Boys, and that he would probably *never* be good and docile and obedient. He voiced his contempt vociferously. It made him popular among his classmates, but it didn't make him like school, and it didn't make him happy. Both of us hated school, which didn't seem to have anything to do with what either of us was, or what either of us wanted.

Remembering those days, when my own children were small I looked around for a noncoercive, noncompetitive school, where the uniqueness of each child would be honored, and where teachers were not dread authorities but people who actually liked kids. (I remember the shock I sustained one Saturday morning when I was twelve and saw a forbidding teacher trundling a laundry cart down the street; I'm sure it had never occurred to me that those people who had so much power over my life—who existed, it seemed, solely in order to be able to torment me—had lives and needs of their own outside the classroom. It certainly never occurred to me that they might occasionally have dirty socks or underwear that needed, prosaically, to be laundered. I thought of this with amusement one day when I visited my son's classroom, and Josh's teacher—a woman as pleasant and understandable as daily bread—casually said, "I'm going to the bathroom and I'd like some privacy." My public-school teachers *never* went to the bathroom, or if they did, they certainly didn't let anyone know about it.)

What I wanted was a school where my children would be happy; I wanted schooling that would respond to their individual natures and needs. It will be apparent that I had zealously read the works of radical educators—Neil, Goodman, Tolstoy, Holt, all of whom proclaimed that good education meets the singular needs of each child. I thought I had found the happy place I wanted in Woodward.

Woodward is an independent, nonsectarian, parent-staff cooperative. The school is maintained through tuition funds (in 1972,
tuition costs ranged from $1625 for nursery to $1925 for eighth
grade), through gifts, and through the limited funds the PTA is
able to raise. Parents may apply for and receive tuition grants on
the basis of financial need; in this way, the school is kept from
being a preserve of the liberal well-to-do. In 1972, five full grants
were extended to inner-city children; a score of children, black
and white, received partial grants.

An innovative educational philosophy that does not rigidly
dichotomize between playing and learning draws children
to Woodward from the upper-middle-class homes of Brooklyn
Heights, as well as from the middle-class (many Woodward parents—artists, teachers, doctors, white-collar workers, civil servants, small-businessmen—owe their presence in Brooklyn to the
brownstone-renovation migration from Manhattan), and from
the working class (the trend seems to be for more and more non-
professionals—blue-collar workers, factory and transit workers—
to enroll their children at Woodward). One of the nice things
about the school, which doesn't rate high on anybody's snob list,
is that it's impossible to tell from observing Woodward's casually
dressed children what their social and economic status is. (Children, it must be said, have a way of working such things out; my
nine- and ten-year-old children report to me on the relative
affluence of each of their classmates, using, as a guide, the size
and style of the birthday parties their friends have. They judge
correctly about fifty percent of the time . . . and in any case, it
doesn't appear to be of more than momentary interest to them.)

Both counter-culture young parents and more staid Establishment types are comfortable at Woodward, where knowledge is
not considered a consumer commodity, bought by discipline and
drills. "Learning" is not something a child is "taught." The children are participants in a process where a teacher is as much a
catalyst for the development of the children's potential as an
instructor. The school pioneered interaging—a concept adapted
from the British "infant schools" (first- and second-graders, and
third- and fourth-graders share a classoom and a teacher)—and
does not grade pupils or issue report cards. Homework, for most
Woodward children, who do not learn by rote, is an exotic activ-

ity engaged in by their public-school friends; the pleasures and ardor of research, however, are familiar even to first-graders. (My son, asked what his favorite thing to do at Woodward was, replied, "Choosing what to do is my favorite thing to do.")

Woodward is, and always has been, interracial. In 1972, forty percent of the school's 290 enrolled children were black. While Woodward, like any successful institution, tends to stand on its laurels and recite past successes in a litany of self-praise, the school—nudged and prodded by an energetic Black Studies Committee—is taking an increasingly active part in the community (largely black) in which its building stands. The school has joined the Pratt Area Community Council (Pratt University, a liberal arts school of art and architecture and a close neighbor, provides Woodward with many of its student teachers) as a vehicle for joint community ventures.

Woodward is a cooperative. But the exact nature of the "cooperative" eludes many parents in spite of corporation by-laws, transcripts of board of trustees' meetings, and mimeographed material, with which we are all regularly inundated, most of which is unreadable, and for the most part, unread. Gertrude Goldstein, the school's director, says that parents have a "voice in education, but not a vote." This has a fine sound to it, but at times—as both the Black Studies Committee and the Sex-roles Committee can testify—it's difficult to see how it works out in practice. Parents do not always know how to channel grievances, for although individual teachers are almost always available to parents, parents have not always felt that communication with the administration was easy, or even that their participation in their children's education was welcome. Some find themselves forced to conclude that whether or not the staff is responsive to complaints and suggestions about curriculum, educational practices, and teachers hinges on the individual parent's style. Unquestionably, some people always seem to make headway with the school's administrators, some claim that they never do, and some never try. Ms. Goldstein has been frank enough to say that the grievances of black parents and those of feminists have occasionally provoked an irritated response: "Why don't they leave us alone to run the school?" She also maintains that the staff are "their own severest critics." I know a lot of parents who would, putting themselves in the running, dispute that.

Still, most Woodward parents send their children to Woodward because it is a happy place—not a perfect place, and not one whose philosophy or staff delights all of the parents all of the time (there are always any number of parents in exceedingly verbal distress over one thing or another)—but a happy place for children, nevertheless.

So much is this true that when, in the beginning of the 1970–1971 school year, a number of feminists invited parents to join the newly formed Sex-roles Committee—in order, they said, to explore ways in which the school might be perpetuating stereotypical sex roles, and reflecting the culture of a sexist society in which females are molded to be passive, submissive, supportive, domestic, powerless, and, somewhat more to the immediate point, rotten at science and math—the response was largely one of aggrieved bewilderment: "You're not suggesting that girls are discriminated against at Woodward? I don't believe it." "Woodward doesn't even force our second-graders to read or our eighth-graders to study algebra. You can't mean that teachers determine what's appropriate behavior for boys and what's appropriate behavior for girls and then force them into those roles?" "You're seeing chauvinism where there isn't any. You're just looking for trouble. Why change a good thing? The whole idea of Woodward is that teachers respond to the needs of the individual child. Nobody's laying anything on those kids. They're happy there."

And so it seemed.

Even the school building itself is a happy one that doesn't scream *Institution* at you. It makes approach unintimidating.

Most urban schools are decaying gothic grotesqueries, or concrete ticky-tacky boxes that begin to look old and mournful almost as soon as they're put up, their implacably bland façades invitations to vandalism. Woodward's children are housed in a Civil War mansion on Brooklyn's Clinton Hill, a preponderantly black neighborhood where newly renovated brownstones stand next to crumbling rooming houses and Mitchell Lama urban-renewal apartment complexes. The 1870s limestone building—once the home of a prosperous sea captain—has a pleasant, expansive disposition. Inside, children's art and papier maché

dinosaurs, bold Stop-the-War manifestos, and goofy graffiti co-
exist happily under noble ceilings with antique bronze lighting
fixtures and carved lintels. Contemporary "tree houses" share
parlor-floor space with massive walnut sliding doors, in a juxta-
position as charming as it is surprising. The building is full of
odd turns and corners and whimsical flights of stairs that termi-
nate in unexpected rooms. It is a place in which one can imagine
having delicious fantasies, or being languorous or zippy or secret
or sad—but not a place that lends itself to rigid discipline or
regimentation; it is too quirky for that: it is a building with a
sense of humor—something about it rebuffs pomposity.

Where functional extensions have had to be built on, as the
school (established in 1959 and dedicated—as the brochure says
—"to the principles of racial and economic integration as well as
to that of individualized education") expanded, the children
have enlivened the boring cinder-block and plaster walls with gay
wall murals; the newer parts of Woodward have a look of somewhat rakish improvisation.

What goes on in the classrooms often seems improvised too.

Gertrude Goldstein, highly respected as a pungent and nurturing intellectual woman, likes to say that Woodward is "flexible
but structured." Adjectives used to define a school's philosophy or
style are, of course—like adjectives in a real-estate ad—practically useless. The children are "free," Ms. Goldstein says, "to do
their own thing—within limits." Now words like "freedom" and
"limits" are to semanticists and metaphysicians like candy on a
summer's day to a baby; they keep you busy for hours, and
dealing with them usually results in a gooey mess; which is why,
no doubt, disgruntled Woodward parents often complain that
there are as many meetings in a school year to worry away at
what these words ought, in actual practice, to mean, as there are
children in the school. "Humanist," another word used to define
Woodward, is like a prepackaged Christmas stocking; you never
know what you're going to find.

What one actually does find at Woodward is something like this:
one's first impression, standing in a hall alive with art and
children, is of constant, undirected movement, of voices and bod-

ies meeting and touching as kids pour out of doors, fling greetings over their shoulders, stop to grab a hand, to whisper a secret, to laugh, or to shout a salutation.

A sixth-grade classroom offers a blackboard on which are printed the children's individual social-studies choices: women's fashions, Eskimos, drugs, primitive tribes, Declaration of Independence, crime, prehistoric man, citizenship, Africa, pollution, Women's Lib, the Middle Ages. As the kids settle in, the teacher looks over some book reports—several children have submitted drawings illustrating highlights of the books they've chosen, in lieu of written reports. "If a child can find expression more freely in art than in words," the teacher says, "why not?"

In my daughter's room, first-graders list "I wonders" on oaktag: "I wonder how the seeds got in the plant." "I wonder how everything everything began." "I wonder if the President will stop the war because say you want to drive a truck instead of fight you wouldn't like it." "I wonder what we're having for dinner." My daughter, Anna, shows me her social studies notebook; the result of a week of study consists of one sentence: "I would not like to live in the early days and been an Indian. Because in a teepee I wouldn't have any privacy." Anna's teacher is comforting two children—one who was hit, and the other who did the hitting.

Next door a harried teacher is waving a bunch of comic books in her hand, in a room that looks as though it contains all the debris from her thirteen students' attics. "No war toys," she calls out over the din. "Will somebody check these to see if they're OK?" The children are holding a white-elephant sale, proceeds to go to UNICEF. "How much money do you think the little kids will bring?" one child asks another.

"What their teacher tells them," a child replies.

"What do you mean? The teacher can't tell them."

"I bet she can, because what if one kid brings a quarter and another kid brings a dollar, the other kid'll feel bad."

My son finds me in a hallway. Josh's second-grade class has been sheltering and feeding a stray cat that wandered into Woodward's playground. Can he take it home? He wants me to be sure not to miss the five-foot loom his third-grade friends have made. And will I drop by his classroom to see his "all about foetuses book that I wrote," and would I have lunch with him, because he's made some cranberry bread. . . . I think of how he once described his school day: "First we work for a half hour [he means reading, writing, arithmetic], then the rest of the day we learn [he means block-building, carpentry, painting, 'Life of Slaves research,' acting, talking, and playing]."

In one corner of the teachers' lunchroom a boy and a girl knead whole wheat bread as they discuss subjects for the monthly Town Hall meeting (for grades 3 to 8; attendance voluntary): "Can the school provide bike storage for students who want to bike to school?" "Why can't we bring our own food? Why aren't there more choices?" In another corner, three girls, one boy, and a student teacher work with vegetable dyes and wax to make Ukrainian-style decorated eggs.

Next door in the science room, where the sharp smell of acid mixes pleasantly with the musty, fecal smell of small animals (guinea pigs, mice, a rabbit), children are doing things with straws and colored-liquid glass jars—"air-pressure experiment," the teacher calls out.

In Ms. Goldstein's office: several seventh-graders come in with a poster and a petition. The poster, hand-lettered by the kids, proclaims: FIGHTING FOR PEACE IS LIKE FUCKING FOR VIRGINITY. Ms. Goldstein had earlier removed the poster from the front hall where the children had prominently displayed it (with the consent of their teacher), after a staff meeting had arrived at the consensus that the obscenity was threatening to younger children, offensive to some teachers, and probably a turn-off for visitors. The kids, irate, are petitioning to put their poster back where they think it belongs. During the discussion that follows, Ms. Goldstein leaves no doubt that the final decision is in her hands: "The whole world is not where you're at," she says, and she begins to question the appropriateness of equating war with sex. Pretty soon the kids are rapping about the relationship between sex and violence, a discussion which seems to interest them more than the immediate issue of their right to display the poster. They leave to report back to their classmates.

In the attic, which smells of sawdust and early summer and the

winey maple whose branches lean over the trellised widow's
walk, a group of boys and girls happily hammer and saw under
the supervision of a slight young Japanese woman.

In a quiet third- and fourth-grade classroom children are poring over math notebooks, or reading the books they have chosen
from the library. The children who read well work with their
friends who read more slowly, helping them patiently and being
attended to solemnly. In this room are children whose reading
skills vary from second-grade level to sixth. Each child is given a
math notebook that suits his or her speed and competence. They
move from green to yellow to red math books as their ability
increases, and once in a while one hears a voice: "I'm almost
through with yellow, now." Some children are practicing script.
Others are dictating stories to their friends who write better. In
their midst, her head almost level with their own, a teacher sits at
a low desk, working with a child who says he feels "stupid
today."

In the playground, fifth-graders are playing soccer.

Eighth-graders, pursuing their elective courses, are making
stage-sets to scale, cutting film to the accompaniment of a Dylan
record, or typing (erasers allowed). An eleven-year-old boy who
has, with grim pragmatism, chosen algebra as an elective, writes
a poem:

> *I hate math*
> *But which way can I go?*
> *How can I escape from it?*
> *How, how I need it*
> *Sure. But not that much.*

A classmate, inspired by his example, writes a poem of her
own:

> *Most pain is double*
> *Every day you have pain*
> *When you do you have trouble*
> *If you don't you're just insane.*
> *The first fear is the first gulp of air.*

It takes a strenuous denial of the evidence of one's senses to
argue that children are not enjoying Woodward.

Parents, however, while acknowledging that they are on to a good thing, find themselves frequently in a state of disenchantment. There are some parents, for example, who disagree with the concept of interaging. They are usually the parents of older children in a group, who fear that their child will be "brought down low," as it were, by his or her more youthful, playful, or unskilled classmates. (Their disenchantment has a limited lifespan, as this year's second-grader in a class of first- and second-graders is next year's third-grader in a class of third- and fourth-graders, whereupon the argument no longer applies.) Then there is always—at meetings—the parent who advances the "But-what-are-you-doing-to-qualify-them-for-the-real-world?" argument. What this parent is complaining of is, ironically, the fact that the children are happy, while the world is not. The world is brutal and competitive and cold; Woodward is nurturing and warm and uncompetitive. The person (usually male) who demands to know what Woodward is doing to "toughen" kids up for the "real world" is sometimes mollified and sometimes not by the suggestion that a child who feels good about herself or himself, who has felt the warmth of adult approval, who is comfortable in his or her own skin, a child who has reveled in the comradeship of friends is probably better prepared for the rigors of the nasty world than a child who feels up against it from the word GO. (One irritated woman, responding to the "Woodward's-too-soft" plaint, said rather snappishly, "Well, what do you want to do about it? Set off bombs under their desks to prove there's a war outside?")

Along these same lines, black parents have occasionally been heard to complain that Woodward children were getting an unreal perspective of the racially tormented world—because white children and black children at Woodward experience little apparent racial strife.

Parents are sometimes bewildered by Woodward's approach to curriculum. Partly because no serial geography or history textbooks are used, many of us have assumed that each teacher merrily (and arbitrarily) planned a year's course of study without regard to what a child may have studied the year before, and that Woodward's approach to social studies was—consequently— eclectic at best. I, for example, found it difficult to believe there was a unified, cohesive study plan when my son, after a six-month fling with dinosaurs in kindergarten, appeared to be studying American Indians in the first, second, and third grades. (When he heard that his fourth-grade teacher planned to build her social studies and arts-and-crafts program around early American settlers, he announced his intention of absenting himself mentally from the proceedings: "I think it's time for me to get terrific at math," because "there were Indians hanging around those settlers, you know.") In fact, there are, Gertrude says, frequent and intensive meetings among staff members to coordinate social-studies programs. In my son's case, it was he who had chosen, merrily and arbitrarily—among a number of choices—to zero in on Indians until he'd had a surfeit of them. (Whether or not a teacher should have stepped in before he reached saturation point, and prevented his Indian-ing himself to boredom, is something else again.) It is also true that Josh studied many things I was not aware of because he didn't share them with me . . . his way of letting me know, no doubt, that school was *his* private world.

Some parents, black as well as white, are beginning to feel that the emphasis on black studies to the exclusion of ethnic minorities is presenting the misleading picture that the world (and Woodward) consists of two groups: blacks, and a white Unitarianlike smoosh. This school year (1972–1973), third- and fourth-graders' social studies revolve around each child examining his or her own ancestry, and considering what brought their forebears to this country, what the immigrants left behind, and how his or her ethnic group interacted with other groups in the New World. One teacher undertook this study course with apprehension, because her family had been plantation slave-owners; after much introspection, she decided that it would be valuable (though painful) for her and the black children—descendants of slaves— to explore the implications of this relationship. It's typical of Woodward that the teacher feeds her own personal experience into discussion and does not distance herself from the subject or from the children. This is a particularly good example, not only of Woodward's response to criticism, but of Woodward's approach to learning—it flows from the child, from the child's experience and perceptions. The feeling is that it is much more meaningful to start with the particular and the unique, and then to generalize outward. This is not, however, to say that education at Woodward is all consider-your-own-navel introspection: teachers make choices—children are not the only ones who may choose—and direct the children's attention outward; it is only to say that the child's own experience is incorporated and utilized as part of the learning process.

Academics present the most difficulties. The theory is that each child learns to read at "his or her own pace," when he or she is "ready." This generally works, although parental heads have been known to turn gray in the process. A child who isn't reading at all in the second grade may suddenly—having found the key and unlocked the mystery—be reading at grade level when he or she gets to third. Parents, implored to be patient, not to get uptight, or put on pressure, are usually rewarded by unharried children who come to learning with love. The teacher's instincts have to be pretty good for this system to succeed, of course, because a child's reasons for not performing are varied and complex. My son, for example, began to make invidious comparisons with his younger sister, whose reading and verbal skills surpassed his. It worried him that he was "dumb." It worried me (I'm one of the parents whose hair started to turn gray) that if he felt inferior he might lose the will to learn. The fact that he has a gorgeous poetic imagination and is a talented artist—and has had full scope to exercise his gifts at Woodward—did not seem sufficient to bolster his ego (and did nothing to allay my fears). I trusted his second- and third-grade teachers, loving women who always made me feel I didn't trust *him* enough, and who insisted that he would soon make the leap into learning. And then one day he read out a long and difficult movie ad from the *Times*. It seemed like magic, a notion he was quick to disabuse me of: "Reading is just hard work. Don't act as if I'm special because I can do that. I just decided I wanted to work, and I worked, and now I can read." He had, in fact, decided it was much more fun to go to art museums (which he loves) if he could read the names of the paintings. In most other schools, he might have been Dick-and-Janed out of that realization of the practical uses to which reading can be put.

The system doesn't always work. Ms. Goldstein's dictum—"We try to encourage children to work to the limits of their ability, and perhaps a little beyond"—sounds good, but like most jargon, it is more useful as a soporific than as a working rule. A few children don't learn to read without tutorial assistance. (The school has—belatedly, some felt—responded to this situation by providing a reading specialist, news that was greeted with a communal sigh of relief.) Woodward is also taking a new look at the problems of the upper grades. The children love their elective courses—who wouldn't?—but they also experience anxieties when it's time for them to enter high school (anxieties which are nothing compared to the ones their parents endure). In 1972, seventh- and eighth-grade parents, feeling that the school's laissez-faire policy was damaging to children about to enter schools with highly accelerated academic programs, had a heavy meeting with Ms. Goldstein and the staff, at which they aired their grievances and their fears. The result was that the staff committed itself to a more vigorous academic program in the upper grades; another good example of the constant renewal and reevaluation that goes on at Woodward.

Interestingly, but not surprisingly, it is the black parents who most often agitate for a more structured, academically oriented program. For many white parents—whose experience has taught them that a diploma is not, necessarily, the way to milk and honey, or even to reasonable contentment—"making it" in the world is no longer synonymous with achieving academic excellence. They can afford to hang loose; their children, being white and therefore privileged, are probably going to make it anyway.

"We have enough Ph.Ds to blow the world up already," Ms. Goldstein is fond of saying. "We need to help people to love one another." Which is all very well, but "love" and doctorates are not necessarily mutually exclusive. Literate people make war; they also make love, and poems, and bread, and music. It seems to some parents that the school, in its noble determination to slay the dragon of competitiveness, may unfortunately be aborting the discipline, habits, and joys of scholarliness as well. I must admit that before the phenomenon of Dr. Kissinger, I—for one— would (naively, perhaps) have thought it unlikely that the finger that pushed the button that dropped the bomb would be that of a scholar.

Which brings us to the heart of the problem facing those of us, like militant blacks and feminists, who work for radical change in a school that is admittedly a happy place.

If, in fact, the school does fulfill its obligation to respond to the true needs and nature of each child, parent pressure groups are redundant. But we all know that our expectations of other people are culturally determined and influenced by our temperamental and class biases and prejudices.

Can a white person really presume to know what a black child "needs"? Can a black child really offer up his or her true "nature" to a white person?

We have preconceived ideas; therefore we misinterpret the evidence. We have been formed by a racist and sexist society, and our perceptions are necessarily filtered through our racist and sexist cultural overlay.

What is a girl's "nature"? It's absurd to believe that we can respond simply and directly to an *individual* girl when we have been conditioned as to how to respond to girls, and what to expect of them, generically. As feminists see it, schools—institutions for socialization within a sexist society—in spite of good intentions, mold children willy-nilly according to societal notions of acceptable behavior. For Woodward to have escaped the all-pervasive "maleness" of our society would be a miracle, just as it would be a miracle for white educators to be totally uncontaminated by racism.

It seemed to feminists that if teachers at Woodward were not fully aware of the subtle as well as the blatant ways in which women are oppressed—if women teachers themselves, having been formed by an educational system oppressive to women, since it incorporates every male myth about women, were not aware of their own oppression—they would continue to mirror society's women-negating attitudes. Our girl children, then, would be victims of their teachers' inertia, and of their teachers' unexamined realities.

But I am not telling it as it was: the Sex-roles Committee did not start from a feminist analysis.

# 2

# Summer 1970:
# A Beginning

> I am a woman in the prime of life,
>     with certain powers,
> and those powers severely limited by
>     authorities whose faces I rarely see.
> —ADRIENNE RICH

> May God be praised for woman
> That gives up all her mind.
> —W. B. YEATS

It was impossible for any woman, in the spring of 1970, not to feel the charge of something very new in the air. The women's Movement was insinuating itself into all our lives. Some of us at Woodward who were later to become part of the Sex-roles Committee were rather frantically repudiating the tenets of feminism, or what we imperfectly understood to be the ideology of feminism, while others of us were engaged in a fearful, tentative flirtation with ideas that threatened, too much, to change us. Some women were cultivating feminism almost as one would a secret but thrilling vice—reading Movement literature, listening to Movement spokeswomen, and viscerally responding but publicly disavowing any connection with "those crazies"; others had forged their way to some kind of honesty, acknowledging their pain without having the political consciousness to know what to do about it. A very few of us were Movement women.

One thing was probably true of all of us: we were beginning to talk to one another in a way we never had before; we were beginning to take ourselves seriously, as women. After all, here was all the world talking about us, discussing our "roles," our femininity, or lack of it, and our happiness. It was disturbing and it was heady. "Women's talk" suddenly took on a new dignity. We were discovering, for example, that all those hours we spent on the phone—and how men hate our telephone talk, trivializing it as "gossip"; how itchy it makes them—were a way of reaching out of our isolation, were a sharing and a caring, however blunted in expression. And suddenly the women's Movement, whether we denigrated it or not, was telling us not to be afraid. So we became less miserly, less superficial, and less guarded in our talk. There had always been an element of peril in "women's talk," a fear of being found out, of being betrayed. But we were all beginning to learn that we had so much more to gain than to lose by making ourselves vulnerable to one another; we began to care very much what other women were thinking and feeling. We were groping our way to new definitions of self, and the identities of other women suddenly became of tremendous concern.

That was how the Sex-roles Committee started—with "women's talk."

In April 1970, toward the end of a PTA Educational Policy meeting that was fairly rancorous and more than usually tense (the latter part of the meeting had been given over to a discussion of drugs, and what with some parents adopting a hipper-than-thou stance and others indulging in the self-righteousness of the abstinent we were all rather eager to go home to bed), a woman stood up and asked a question no one was prepared to entertain:

"What differences, if any," Andrea Ostrum asked Gertrude Goldstein, "do you see between the way girls and boys function at school, and how do you account for them? Is Woodward dealing with sex-role discrimination?" It was, some of us later reported having felt, an alarming and disturbing question—but not, at the time, an energizing one. Gertrude, in a rather dilatory fashion, observed that by the time children reached junior high school boys were far better than girls at math, and that, she implied, was that. Maia Scherrer, a first- and second-grade teacher, immediately declared herself "an old-line feminist from way back," and went on to observe that her first- and second-grade girls were just not interested in things like rockets. "Well, they're interested when you get them alone," she admitted, "but they're reluctant to express their interest in front of boys." With that (in spite of Andrea's mumbled "atrocious!") both the meeting and the question of sex-role discrimination fizzled out.

The issue, however, continued to have a kind of half-life as a few women attempted to revive it at grade meetings with individual teachers. Almost invariably, the teacher's response was that although group dynamics varied, no troubling differences between boys and girls had been observed. There were exceptions, however. Maia Scherrer said that for ten years she'd been observing that girls' perceptions of phenomena were sensory, while boys were concerned with the way things functioned. Maia deplored this dichotomy, believing that it implied disaster for girls' intellectual growth. A teacher whose inclination is always to prod kids and help them stretch, she likes engaging very young children with concepts, and dislikes complacency of any sort, yet her attitude then suggested that this difference was more or less an unfortunate fact of life. (Maia now directs a day-care center, and having always dealt very forthrightly and energetically with racial problems, she has found from her day-care experience with a group of white working-class children that class differences present as much of a problem as race. When, for example, she encouraged her middle-class teachers to spend part of a day making a forthcoming solar eclipse comprehensible to three- and four-year-olds, they responded that "these children don't need to know about that kind of thing." They evidently considered the subject too lofty for working-class children. It is interesting to see how, in a context other than that of sexism, teachers' expectations govern their perceptions of a child's "needs.")

Gertrude Goldstein and Ruth Fishman (the director of Woodward's lower school) were beginning to get scuttlebutt from the grade meetings, and what they heard didn't exactly exhilarate them. Gertrude confesses that she was "mildly irritated." She was very frank about it: "Sometimes I just see parents as nuisances," she said, "The sex-roles thing kept surfacing, but I really thought it would go away."

It seemed likely that it would "go away." Women were used to speaking up for their children; but when they spoke of sex roles, they were also speaking for themselves. They were addressing themselves as women to a problem that was essentially a women's problem (we may choose to define it as a "human" problem, but the fact remains that the cry to liberate women did not swell up from the ranks of men, and men weren't raising it at Woodward, either). Women were speaking out of a burgeoning awareness of their own oppression and their own necessities. And women are just not used to speaking up for themselves. Even when they were zealous, determined, and intrepid, individual women could always be dismissed—as in fact they were—as eccentric or atypical, or as nuisances.

Yet in spite of the fact that there was no organized meeting of minds and wills, Woodward women were very busy talking with one another, sharing their observations and perceptions.

In June, school broke for summer vacation. Andrea Ostrum had experienced feminism as a sudden illumination. (Her husband, Hirsch Grunstein, well remembers the night when a feminist writer and Redstocking "radicalized" his wife: "Goddammit," he thought, "this is going to be trouble." His reaction was tragicomic; the first step to liberation is often a step away from the kitchen range, and Hirsch could see it coming: although he later became a feminist himself, his first gut reaction to Andrea's conversion was, "And I hate to cook!" He envisioned a martyrdom of endless evening meals.) In July, still troubled by what she considered Woodward's implicit sexist stance, Andrea called together a group of neighboring Woodward mothers—who were in New York for the summer—for an informal rap group. Andrea and several others had been in consciousness-raising groups and by then were declared feminists; those who were not had two things in common: they had daughters at Woodward, and they were aware of a kind of subliminal distress, inchoate feelings that all was not well in their daughters' school world.

The women who attended that first meeting describe it as both warm and exciting; they felt very close to one another as they shared anecdotes about what they'd observed at Woodward, and discussed their own girlhood educations. They felt, although they were all at very different places, the exhilaration that comes with the first stirrings of common purpose.

I was not present at that meeting, nor, in all likelihood, would I have gone if I had been invited. I was at the time stubbornly committed to the naive (and masochistic) notion that the great thing was to solve all one's problems alone, with no help, with no expectation of solace from any quarter. That summer, my children were in India, visiting their father, from whom I had been divorced for two years; I was having a lacerating time with an extremely neurotic man whose eccentricities perversely held me to him. (Stendahl says that all a man has to do to endear himself to a woman is to wear an overcoat in the summer; this man wore a suit of spiked armor. I was, with complete lack of realism, determined to get through to the loving inno-cent I believed—on no evidence at all—dwelt within.) Out of a complicated pride, and out of some kind of romantic-arrogant-adolescent vision of myself as a lonely doomed-to-be-misunderstood sufferer, I was unwilling to talk to other women about my pain. It took a really brutal summer, and lots of covert reading of feminist literature (and the return of my healthy, commonsensical children) to convince me that other women could help me to understand my own experience, which I had been determined to see as singular and unique. In fact what happens when women get together in consciousness-raising groups—and what happened to the women who formed the nu-cleus of the Sex-roles Committee—is a recognition that neither our diversity nor our singularity negates the fact that we are members of a class (or a caste) and that the commonality of our experience derives from our being members of the same op-pressed class. There is nothing frightening in that (although, jealous of my singularity, it threw me into a panic to think of myself becoming one of many); it doesn't necessitate sacrifice of one's personhood or assimilation into an undifferentiated mass. It is ultimately reassuring, because it means, not that one "gives oneself" to a cause, but that one finds oneself among different-alike, struggling others. I was not ready to understand, that sum-mer, that to declare oneself a feminist is not to deny existential loneliness, but merely to acknowledge that women can, in many ways, help one another, because their common experience enables them to understand one another in ways men and women often cannot. I was terrified to think that I might have to submerge my own voice in some kind of feminist chorus; I did not understand that there did not have to be an aggressively feminist point of view about everything from childbirth to Yoko Ono's art, but that women—for certain purposes—might band together to secure recognition of their rights without having to speak in a single polemical voice. The women present at that meeting in July were far ahead of me. They were beginning to understand that a communal sharing of pain may lead to a political analysis, which may, in turn, lead to a revolution within one's life (and thus to a dedication to a radical change in society).

Aside from Andrea Ostrum (who was then Andrea Grunstein, having not yet reverted to the use of her unmarried name)—a clinical psychologist, then working toward her doctorate, and caring, with her husband, Hirsch, for their three children—among the women present at that meeting were Mimi Anderson, a painter (the mother of a boy and a girl, Mimi had not painted enough to satisfy her since her marriage—to a painter); Adrienne Yurick, who had long been active in radical politics and who now teaches in a community cooperative nursery school (she and her husband Sol have a daughter at Woodward); Brett Vuolo—the mother of a boy and a girl—who had, before her marriage, been an actress, and who, at the time of the meeting, described herself as a "housewife" (Brett and Mimi both now work at radio station WBAI as heads of the Drama-Literature Department); Mimi Meyers, a photographer (who is now in graduate school, and sharing, with her husband Bart, a teacher, the duties of the house and the care of their young daughter); Peggy Sandback, who then saw her identity as "housewife," and has now returned to school; Cora Lynne David (who was then beginning to become interested in video taping, an interest she was later actively to pursue); and Vivian Ubell—who has a particular aversion to being asked "What do you do?" because implicit in that question is the assumption that if you're a housewife (Vivian has two sparkling daughters whom she likes a lot) you don't *do* anything. (Vivian, who is now working toward a degree in social work, told me this story: when she was in college, she wanted very much to be a nurse. Her counsellors were horrified; they said nursing was for "dumb" girls—and they proceeded to suggest all kinds of alternatives—teaching, for example, and social work. What they never suggested—and what never occurred to her—was that she might become a doctor. She is still toying with the idea of becoming a nurse. It's interesting that nursing, once a field closed to women, began to be demeaned as soon as it became almost the exclusive province of women.)

These women had much in common. They were all married, all white, and they all had children at Woodward. But their backgrounds differed (working-class, middle-class, upper-middle-class), and so did their styles: some were earnest, some were convivial and extroverted, some were garrulous, others shy. Everyone of them remembers the evening as remarkable for the insights the frank sharing of past lives produced. Now, anyone who's been in therapy can testify to the illusive, unrecapturable nature of "insight." What seems like dynamite news to the person who's been enlightened often sounds banal—*but everybody knows that already*—when repeated to someone else. Similarly, critics of the women's Movement have occasionally voiced irritation over the "triviality" of awakening feminists'· insights into their condition. But, just as psychoanalytic insights are of tremendous value to the patient (who didn't, in her or his gut, "know that already"), the initial stirrings of a feminist consciousness seem, to the individual awakening, like the beginning of a redemption from a life of lies. We start with our own pain, and we authenticate it by sharing it with other women. We don't all begin by speaking in the accents and with the style of Simone de Beauvoir (probably even Simone de Beauvoir doesn't always talk like Simone de Beauvoir).

Peggy Sandback, who describes herself as a "nontalker," said she kept feeling little thrills of doubt and alarm: "I'm afraid of this. What if my son should turn out to be homosexual?" She also kept obdurately repeating to herself, "I won't deny my daughter pretty long dresses." Nevertheless she felt that "almost everything anyone said was like a light turning on." (Peggy continued, throughout the life of the Sex-roles Committee, to question—very softly, but also steadfastly—the effect even minor changes of direction and emphasis would have on her daughter's psyche and sense of self. She needed to feel that her child's serenity was not going to be violated by militant insistence on feminist "norms." Her concern for long dresses was symbolic; months after, when many of the rest of us were expressly concerned with the concepts of male and female intellectuality and aggression, she was wondering aloud what the consequences of an androgynous approach to learning would be on romantic love when our children reached puberty. . . . In her own life, despite some early qualms and misgivings about what liberating children from sex roles might do to the cosmic order of things—i.e., to Love—she made some dramatic changes: several months after the Sex-roles Committee began, she determined to return to school for a Master's degree in social work. She has never ceased to question, however, with great sensitivity, all the implications of adults' changing values and making those changes known to their children.)

Brett Vuolo, who smiles wryly at her proclivity to see the other side of a question—any question—remembers spending that night in an orgy of *yes, buts*: "I agreed with equal pay for equal work, what fool wouldn't? And I suppose I agreed in general with all the reformist principles of the Movement, *yes, but* I thought my problems were personal, individual and neurotic. . . . I felt I was the author of my own oppression, *yes, but* men are oppressed too. I thought feminism had nothing to say to me, *but* I had a nagging feeling that I might be limiting my daughter's options. I hadn't even begun to think in terms of what women's liberation might do to my son."

Brett says she was just beginning to be aware of the terrible life she had created out of a so-called privileged childhood, which had seemed "perfectly rotten" to her. "My mother had a successful career," she said, "so I created a life in opposition to everything I thought she stood for, and it was a mess." Sent away to boarding-school in the third grade, she had there been pushed to the limits of her talents, and in spite of her love and admiration for the headmistress (spinster and celibate), she was determined to stay at home and be a middle-class housewife, no more, no less. She admitted that she had gone to the meeting feeling very detached, but that she had some not-too-well-formulated feelings that something was being "put on" her daughter. She wanted to do something for her: "I seemed to be inflicting my values (which weren't making *me* as happy as a clam) on her, and I wondered if the school was doing the same thing." She described the evening as "so warm and *nice*; I didn't feel isolated; I knew no one would despise me." It made her think of how pleasant it must have been in the days when women sat and talked together, and quilted: "I found I just loved the idea of being with other women and talking about women."

Interestingly, when Brett became an active feminist, she began to put most of her energies into unearthing women's revealed history. She has been able to find unpublished diaries of colonial and pioneer women, and has used them as a basis for several shows she has produced for radio station WBAI.

Snatches of the women's personal reminiscences—some bemused, some funny, some bitter—have been reported to me:

"I remember feeling it was OK to be good in English," one woman said, "but horrible to be good in math, and I had to pretend to hate science. History was sort of up for grabs. . . . It was touch and go whether you could allow yourself to be good at it or not."

Another woman remembers being "terrific at everything. I don't really think I suffered from being 'smart' in high school," she said. "Boys still asked me out, I mean. Never anybody like the football captain, of course, just the boys who were smarter than I was." (It appears to be an immutable law of cultural life that boys don't date girls who are "smarter" than they are—which leads to all the *Seventeen*-magazine dissembling that girls become so adept at: "Ask him about his hobbies, his interests; let him know you admire him, and never let him know you're smarter than he is." An accomplished woman is obliged to marry a man who is even more accomplished than she—which limits her choice considerably; a great man may marry whom he likes.)

I know, from my own high-school experience, what it means to feel that you're the kind of girl that's never going to get a tumble from the football captain (this may be a feeling engendered from having grown up in the fifties; perhaps now the classy thing is to date the poetry editor of the high school yearbook . . . the fact remains that young girls judge themselves by the men who select—or reject—them). When I was in high school I won lots of medals, and a coveted scholarship to a good university . . . and

then one day, in the hall, somebody mistook me for a cheerleader. It is no exaggeration to say that this mistake made me
happier than I'd ever been. No accolade from my teachers, and
no academic reward, meant anything to me compared to being
mistaken for a cheerleader. . . .

The women's resentments, as expressed at that meeting, took
varied forms:

One woman said, "Everybody was always telling me to look
nice. So I'd spend hours and hours putting goo on my face,
twisting my hair in steel curlers, using lemon rinses and beer
rinses . . . once I used a depilatory on my face and burned myself
so badly I couldn't go to school for a week. But all those people
who were always telling me to look nice always made fun of me
for doing that stuff to myself, and they used to say I was con-
ceited."

"My father owned a business," another woman said; "he used
to tell me how proud he was of 'his girl,' and he used to say I
could *do* anything, or *be* anything I wanted . . . except, of course,
work in the business. That was reserved for my younger brother.

"I used to be a 'tomboy,' and I couldn't understand why all at
once I was told to stop playing ball with the boys," she continued. "It was about the time I got my first period, I guess. As
for 'girls' basketball rules,' that kind of thing filled me with rage.
I was as good as any boy, only I was never allowed to prove
it.

"When I won a scholarship, my father said, 'Well, that's nice,
but you don't really need it. Your brother is the one who has to
make his way in the world.' "

These are not merely the disgruntled comments of women who
do not choose to remember that only a blessed few adults—male
or female—remember childhood as a happy place. It's significant
that the thread that runs through all their rememberings is their
perception, as girls, that there was something rare and wonderful
and mysterious about being a boy, that boys were engaged in
growing outward into the world, while they were locked ("pro-
tectively") into a stifling, claustrophobic place. To say this, is not
to indulge in maudlin self-pity, but to understand how we have
become what we are (and, hopefully, to transcend what we are).
The messages girls receive are very different from those boys

receive. For example, when I was little and asked my father for money, he would play a little game: he'd smile and say, "Beg a little." When my brother asked for money, he was told to work for it. My father loved us both, but he firmly believed that my brother would have to work for what he got, while I—a girl— would always be in a dependent ("begging") position.

Many Sex-roles committeewomen report similar experiences They all felt trapped in a double-bind. Some were expected to perform brilliantly at school . . . and then told not to be smart or "fresh" when they "showed off." (Girls, as Margaret Mead points out, are "un-sexed" by success; boys are "un-sexed" by failure.) While feminists often stress the indisputable fact that boys are pressured to achieve, it isn't really as simple as that. Many Woodward feminists find their experience compares with mine: whatever I did was *expected* of me—because I was a girl. I was *supposed* to be good and smart. But whatever I did was also *inessential*. A son is something miraculous. Boys are expected to achieve; girls are expected to conform. Boys are also forgiven when they do not achieve; they are permitted to rebel—the prodigal is always a son. There is something in their very Being that excites wonder. As one Woodward woman said, "I was Number Two—I always had to try harder. Any little thing my brother did was remarkable. I mean, I could do everything that was required of me and be smart and good and make the beds and clean my room and still I never heard that radiance in my parents' voices that they had when they spoke of my brother. I was always the responsible one, responsible for the house and responsible for him, while my brother just seemed to have to *be*. I plodded." Daughters are not permitted to be rebellious. I can illustrate this from my own experience: once my brother played hooky on the first day of spring; someone took his picture in Central Park, and it appeared in the evening papers. He was yelled at when he got home, but there was an edge of pride in my parents' voices even as they ritually scolded. If *I* had done that, my parents would have been bitterly ashamed. My brother was always in trouble, and always expected to be.

While boys' sexuality is often blunted (by parents' inordinate attention to masturbation, for example), they are always *assumed to be* sexual creatures. Girls are not thought of as sexual beings; their role is to react (as well as to be acted upon). Girls understand very early that they are the guardians of sexual morality, their own—and that of boys. They must fend off the sexuality it is taken for granted boys will express. I remember my first sexual experimentation, when I was five, with Billy-down-the-block. There was the usual mutual giggly exploration of bodies, we kissed, and (most fascinating of all) we watched each other urinate. We got caught. Nobody got very mad at Billy, who was—after all—doing what boys are expected to do: "That's the way boys are," my mother said. I was taught it was my job not to let that happen.

If girls are not thought of as "naturally sexual," they are thought of as "naturally religious" (their nature is spiritual, boys' nature is animal—no wonder men fear and despise the "superior" creatures who are punished for their presumed spiritual superiority). My mother was active in a fundamentalist religion, against which my brother (with great good sense) rebelled when he was very young. He was exempted from religious obligations (although never without the hope that he would, like the prodigal, eventually—and with great rejoicing—return). I had to conform. A rebellious son was tolerated, but not a rebellious daughter. From my parents' attitudes toward sex and toward religion, I received conflicting messages: I learned that it was easier for girls to be pure and righteous, but I learned also that girls were dirty and if they didn't worship and conform, terrible things would happen to them. None of the Sex-roles committee-women's experience exactly paralleled my own, but each of them reports having received exactly the same conflicting messages. As a consequence, almost all of the women I spoke with suffer from virulent forms of guilt. ("I still apologize to my family when it rains," one woman said.) Psychological studies have shown that, while adult males are likely to experience shame—dishonor, a loss of reputation or esteem—adult females are more likely to experience guilt—a sense of having sinned, a feeling, unattached to a specific cause, of being culpable of an unknown, but terrible, offense. (Boys are afraid of being caught, or found out; girls—heirs to Eve's trashing of innocence—dwell in the conviction that they are guilty of Original Sin.)

Feminists have been dismissed as "dissatisfied women," as if to be dissatisfied were proof of the illegitimacy of their cause. Well, of course feminists are dissatisfied—one doesn't set about liberating oneself from satisfaction and fulfillment. But the women who formed the nucleus of the Sex-roles Committee were proceeding from more than their own newly articulated dissatisfactions, from more than a remembrance of things past. The sharing of childhood experience was only one part of that meeting in July, 1970. The women also talked about what they had observed at Woodward that gave them cause for concern. Among the things that came under their scrutiny were Woodward's curriculum, library and textbooks, the physical setup of nursery and kindergarten classrooms, and parent-staff relations.

*Books:* Woodward's library reflected the overwhelming "maleness" of children's books, in which boys celebrate life by living it fully and reaching out to the world, and girls reach out to boys. Early-childhood readers celebrated stereotypical nuclear-family roles: mothers and girls stay home and clean, fathers go off to work, and boys have adventures. Not only is this demeaning and cruelly limiting, it does not even accurately reflect childen's reality. For instance, many Woodward mothers work, and many are professionals, yet one of the few textbooks (a first-grade reader) that showed a woman working placed her in her daughter's school cafeteria—cooking.

*Physical Setup of Nursery and Kindergarten Classrooms:* Heavy blocks, trucks, and carpentry equipment were in one well-defined section, while "dress-ups," dolls, and homemaking equipment were in another. The boys obviously considered the heavy "doing" stuff their turf, and when a girl wandered over to the carpentry table she was easily intimidated and likely to be shut out, making crossing over the invisible boundary line between "boys'" things and "girls'" things an emotional impossibility for many children. One woman who had spent a morning in her son's kindergarten class reported that she had seen only one girl (who happened to be dressed in a feather boa, beads, and twelve jangling bracelets) attack the blocks; her determination was as remarkable as her costume.

*Curriculum:* Women are absent from history books; their history is largely unrevealed. Not only emphasis on women's legal and social battles, but a sense of the "dailiness" of their lives —the unique contribution women have made to our civilization—appeared to be missing from the curriculum. For example, children may learn that early American colonists gained experience in self-government; they are not likely to be taught that female colonists were denied the privilege of self-government. They learn that brave pioneers crossed the country in covered wagons with their wives and children and their cattle; little in what they are taught encourages them to think of the women as other than part of the baggage. They read that man climbed out of the trees to hunt, and that he also made pots. There is little in what they read that reminds them that the "man" who made pots was a woman. History is taught literally in terms of "man's" development, and in the very structure of the language teachers use is inherent the idea of man's superiority over woman—the use of the word mankind, for example, when what is meant is humanity, and the automatic use of a male pronoun. (Men who think these linguistic objections are trivial ought to consider what it would do to their world-view—and their egos—if they had been forced to see themselves embraced by the term "womankind," or if they were always to read "she" when a person of either sex was referred to. Language reflects and creates our reality, and it is hard to ignore the fact that English as currently used implies that females are, at best, derivative, and at worst, slightly less than human.)

A good example of the maleness of revealed history is Marcel Ophuls' masterful film, *The Sorrow and the Pity.* This brilliant documentary of the Nazi wartime occupation of a French town was flawed by the almost complete absence of—not just a female "point of view" (whatever that might be)—but of females, period. Toward the end of the film, it is true, we hear from one woman who was accused of being a collaborator, and we are permitted to see women, whose crime had been to sleep with German soldiers, having their heads shaved in retribution (surely a symbolic castration). (It's interesting that male collaborators, however harsh their treatment at the hands of the French, were not forced to wear their shame publicly, as these pathetically vulnerable women were. . . . Men have sneered at feminists for insisting that sex is a "political" act. But they seemed to have thought it was in France after World War II.) With these two exceptions, not once in the four-and-a-half-hour film do we hear what it was like for women during those occupation days. It is as if they had not been there. We hear male Resistance fighters, male Vichy supporters, male apologists for one political view or another. But quite aside from the fact that there were female Resistance fighters and women who endangered their own lives to shelter Allied infiltrators, life did go on; it was not just a succession of guerrilla forays and political accommodations. Women's hearts and minds and bodies were also engaged; they were present, but they are not accounted for. Women had babies under the most miserable conditions. Jewish women and children suffered (Mendés-France was surely not the only Jewish intellectual in that town, though he is the only one interviewed). Women provided the continuity and background against which men performed their noble or ignoble acts. They also—presumably—performed their own noble or ignoble acts. Yet history chooses to spotlight men only. What was it like for women? In this film we are never told. In one scene we see a group of farmers reminiscing about their Resistance activities, while their women stand silently in the background, watchful, and ready to serve. I wanted to know what it was like for these women during those bitter days. I wanted some sense of the dailiness of their lives, their deprivations, their sorrows; but the women never spoke. In wartime women suffer all the anguish of the menfolk, and share little of the exhilaration. In peacetime, their anguish is not judged worthy of note, so we are left with the impression that "real life" must mean political abstractions and overt political acts. What a lopsided view! Similarly, for our children, their study of colonial times, pioneer times, or the Civil War, is likely to treat them to a view of history in which women are notably absent, thus depriving them of both female role-models and the sense of the texture of daily life.

*Parent-staff Relations:* The women wondered what message our children were getting from the roles they saw their mothers and fathers play with regard to their education. Of course, there were men on the Board of Trustees, and when some contact such as a financial undertaking had to be made with the outside world, the call automatically went out to fathers. Fathers did the "important" fundraising, while mothers made casseroles for the school bazaar. (One woman who spent hours and hours baking bread, organizing, and sewing, for a school fundraising bazaar said that she'd worked it out that her time had been worth four cents an hour in terms of funds actually raised. She didn't feel this was so bad, since she preferred baking bread to calling on bank presidents, but what rankled was that her husband had contributed exactly one hour to the bazaar, which resulted in an effusive letter of thanks. She got none. The only implication she could draw was that his work was regarded as essential, while she was *expected* to volunteer.) Men who contributed time or effort to the school were considered extraspecial; the feeling seemed to be that we were privileged to have the advantage of their superior wisdom. Women were expected to work for the school, the assumption being that the children being educated were theirs, and it looked like it, too; even when both parents worked, mothers brought the kids to school, and mothers brought them home at the end of the day. When a child was sick, the mother stayed home, though she might work just as hard, and at as important a job as her husband, outside the home. When there was a problem with a child that necessitated a parent conference, it was invariably the mother who presented herself at school. Ms. Goldstein was frank enough to admit that when a father answered the call for a parent conference, her inclination had been to think, I wonder what's wrong in that household? Education, obviously, is perceived as one of mommy's chores. The exacting, time-consuming, humdrum but necessary mechanics of keeping a school functioning, as opposed to the glamorous tasks, always fell to women. It was always women, for example (often in a panic that they would be late for their own offices), who started round-robin telephone calls in inclement weather to announce that school would be closed. Designated as "class mothers," they often didn't even have names. Class lists identified parents as Mr. and Mrs. John Smith. "What do I call Melissa's mother?" my daughter once asked me, consulting one of these lists. "She doesn't have a name."

As Woodward women began to look at the education of their children from a feminist point of view during the summer of 1970, they began to understand that what was true of society in general—it had been true in their own homes as well—was true of Woodward: our unconscious attitudes toward the sexes, our visceral acceptance of the cultural myth that women are secondary, derivative, complementary beings, had led us to instruct our sons, by suggestion and indirection, that the world was theirs for the grasping, and to "protect" and shelter (and limit and subdue) our daughters.

# 3

# Fall and Winter 1970: Politicizing Feelings

> Hitler burned books.
>
> —MAIA SCHERRER

> These young snips, acting like they're discovering America.
>
> —GERTRUDE GOLDSTEIN

> We had a fantasy we'd go to the staff and blow their minds; we were wrong.
>
> —ANDREA OSTRUM

In the fall of 1970, Woodward women—many of whom had taken the step from articulation of personal pain to political consciousness—began to meet regularly to talk about Woodward and their children's education.

At first, the group was made up of neighborhood friends drawn together on the basis of propinquity: one heard them described as "the bitter Park Slope women" who were doing some silly whining-complaining-agitating about a nonexistent problem. Soon they found they had an audience. Changes had been wrought over the summer; vague discontents had "yeasted," as one woman said. More women were in consciousness-raising groups. Mothers spend a great part of their lives talking to other mothers; and soon the informal network of school-based relationships, and the telephone grapevine established for our children's socializing became vehicles for informal consciousness-raising

among women. The group which had been meeting over the
summer was calling itself a committee by now and had begun
actively to encourage attendance at "Sex-roles Committee" meetings.

No one can remember now why the women chose this rather
awkward and uninspired name, and nobody likes it much. It was
probably chosen because it had a nice, flat, academic tone—it
hardly evoked images of fiery feminists or the mythical bra burn-
ings that were inflaming (or titillating) so many minds, although
there were occasions when it did not have the desired soothing
effect. Often I could practically hear the raised eyebrows of
baby-sitters or teen-age children when I conveyed a sex-roles-
meeting message over the telephone. I'm sure there are still people convinced that it had something to do with orgies.

Meanwhile, more and more people responded to the call (as I
had), and the group broadened. Others, however, continued to
dismiss our concerns as trivial, parochial, or counterlibertarian:
"In this school? Where boys weave and make candles and bake
bread? What more do you want?" Or, "I'm working with the
Black Studies Committee, and I think their demands are more
pressing." Some felt that "these kids are going to have to live in a
world where men and women *do* have definite roles, and they'd
better learn to get used to it," while others absolutely refused "to
be part of a group that wants to impose adult values on children."

Nonetheless, meetings, with an average attendance of about
twelve, began to be held on a regular biweekly basis. The meetings were leaderless and had no agenda. To ensure that the more
verbally aggressive among us did not dominate discussion, those
who wished to speak raised hands, and each speaker, as she
concluded, called upon another woman with an upraised hand.
We felt comfortable with one another.

During those September and October months, we were not
forming a plan of action and deciding how to effect change as
much as rehearsing the evidence of our senses, wondering out
loud how we had allowed our lives and those of our children to
be governed by the unexamined principles of sexism, which now
seemed so sterile and malevolent to us all. . . . We were also
beginning to build up little resentments against the staff because

they hadn't identified the problem before we had. Occasionally we behaved as if we were saying, "We've delivered our children to you and you've betrayed them." Of course we also said that we accepted our share of the blame, but probably *because* we respected Woodward so much, we were aghast that Woodward was still where we had been before our conversion.

Women who later became active in the Sex-roles Committee described to me where they were in their thinking at that time:

Adrienne Yurick had been involved in the women's Movement long before the Sex-roles Committee gained momentum (she had helped to organize "Half of Brooklyn," a group of politically radical feminists). Consequently, she was "tired of talking." Adrienne, whose scrupulous personal integrity and intensity lend to all her undertakings the passion of complete commitment, said she "wanted action." But she could foresee difficulties: "Here we were—radical women, liberals, apolitical, private women—all different in style and ideology, and all at different stages of political consciousness. I wasn't sure how we could get it together." An evolved feminist who had read all the radical literature and gone to more radical conferences than she cared to remember, Adrienne was nevertheless drawn to the Woodward women "who were just beginning to acknowledge their oppression. I had already shared my pain with other women; but I was drawn to the Woodward women because of our mutual concern for our daughters. I began to feel that sharing pain could still be valuable—if we were really prepared to do something about it."

Adrienne's concerns were echoed by others: "How such a diverse group could work together effectively," said one woman, "I wasn't quite sure. And it alarmed me that some people were already seeing the staff as 'The Enemy' because it hadn't taken up the banner first. I'd done enough substitute-teaching to know that telling anecdotes about hammers and nails and blocks and dolls has a limited use. . . . These stories are always subject to different interpretations, and I anticipated that the staff—bound to feel threatened—might be eager to feel that the anecdotes were just a peculiar focus for the anger and bitterness of people who had problems with their kids."

Compare these reminiscences of women who were not, in the fall of 1970, conscious feminists, with those of someone like

Adrienne, and both the difficulties and the exciting positive possibilities of women at different levels of thought working together may be seen: one woman—the mother of a boy and a girl—remembers having been terribly pleased with Woodward because it had not been guilty of "feminizing" her male child; it had not required docility and conformity—female "virtues"—of her active, aggressive son. But she was beginning to question why both she and her son's teacher took pleasure in the fact that "he's all boy . . . he never sits still," while the same attributes in her daughter elicited anxiety and reproach—"What's wrong with her? She can't sit still." She was beginning to monitor and to question all her responses and all the attitudes she had taken for granted, as was another woman, who says of the women's Movement, "I was ripe for it. The Movement had been nickering around in my mind and feminist ideas had lodged themselves there, though I was afraid to admit it. It was all there ready to be put together. . . . I was beginning to ask myself, Is my husband my job? Are my children my job?" She would probably not, she says, have responded to an invitation to go to a women's consciousness-raising meeting, "Because then I'd have been admitting that the Movement had gotten to me; but I could go to a meeting about children, because that's what my life was *supposed* to be about." Another woman remembers spending a lot of time "comparing lives. I'd look at women who worked, and at their kids, and at women who didn't work, and at their kids—I'd try to figure out which was better and who was happier. . . . The only life I *didn't* examine was my own." She felt, she says, "like a comparison shopper in life-styles. If anyone had asked me, I would have defended my own. . . . When my eight-year-old daughter announced to me that she was never going to get married and never going to have babies, I was horrified. I thought she was judging my life—negatively. A year earlier, I'd have dismissed what she said as a childish whim, or a 'phase.' Now, everything anybody said that cast any doubt on my role in the nuclear family alarmed and disturbed me."

The other problem anticipated by some women—that the staff was bound to be perceived as "The Enemy," and that lines were going to be drawn between the "Establishment" and the "insurgents"—is reflected in this woman's comments:

"I hated PTA meetings. They were stilted and boring. I thought all those status-quo ladies were all afraid of really confronting the staff about anything. I'd had occasion to confront the staff, and I found that they were more concerned with jealously preserving their own interests than with fostering mine. The PTA was diffident and deferential. The first Sex-roles Committee meeting I went to was exactly the opposite. It was vital, and everybody was prepared for confrontation."

Barbara Mask, a pleasant, straight-talking black woman, who was wrestling with changes in her own life (an anatomist, she had recently begun to teach at Medgar Evers College after several years' hiatus in her career, and she was also coping with the demands of a new baby), didn't think sexism presented much of a problem at Woodward, nor did she feel, then, that the women's Movement had any application to her own life. She was willing to concede that "the women's Movement was doing something to my head, because I was feeling less and less guilty about being bitchy. Unless you can say that getting bothered at kitchen-type things is feminist, I was not a feminist. But I did allow myself to get angry—like when my husband did the dishes: *What biological reasons can there possibly be for his sloppiness?* I'd think." Her first reaction to the Sex-roles Committee, after attending several meetings, was negative: "I couldn't stand to hear white women talk about their 'oppression.' Hell, when anyone who is free, white, and twenty-one tells me she's oppressed, my reaction is, You have some damned shallow perception of oppression." But she took a kind of detached gleeful pleasure in waiting to see the consequences of feminists' activities: "I thought, It'll be fun to get Gertrude Goldstein involved in this. Having had my own problems with staff responsiveness, both as an individual and as part of the Black Studies group, I sort of wanted to sit back and see what you white people would do with this one."

Carol London, who teaches in the public-school system and who was one of the few early committee members with a child in the upper grades, had another sort of problem, one which sprang from her sense of indebtedness to Woodward: "My daughter had difficulty with skills, and Woodward had gotten her over some bad hurdles. It was hard for me to express discontent because I didn't want to feel disloyal to a school where everyone had worked so hard to make my child happy." Carol also, however, questioned "the school's role in perpetuating my daughter's passivity. My daughter is unassertive. She accepts so much crap without complaint or compunction or griping. I wasn't inclined to blame the school for any of that, but I wasn't sure, on the other hand, whether Woodward was providing her with role-models that made her feel positive about being a girl. It seemed to me that she learned about Indians for a hell of a long time without seeming to know anything about Indian women. I felt that a girl who knew all about the Harlem Four should damn well know about Susan B. Anthony and Sojourner Truth, too." So, in spite of niggling feelings that "any kind of pressure group was in a way disloyal," Carol began to come to meetings.

As for me—I accepted an invitation to attend a Sex-roles Committee meeting in the fall of 1970 largely out of curiosity, and really for no better reason than that I liked the woman—Mimi Anderson—who extended the invitation. I looked forward to the meeting as an occasion for socializing with women I had met at Woodward and liked. I did not personally know any feminists well; and indeed my first contact with feminists, in the spring of 1969, had produced a generally unfavorable effect: I had been laboring in the peace movement; at an organizing meeting in preparation for a Washington march, feminists protested that they would not march under *Women Strike for Peace* banners that proclaimed *Not Our Sons/Not Their Sons*. Their reasons for rejecting that slogan were as obscure to me as their determination was irritating. The events of the march itself, however, were consciousness-raising. Feminists were allowed on the platform begrudgingly; I was moved by their ardor, if not by the substance of what they said. When Pete Hamill's column the next day described the "stirring" speech of antiwar activist David Dellinger and compared it to the "shrill, strident voices" of the women, I was unaccountably annoyed. The Chicago Seven were then standing trial for conspiracy to incite riots across state lines; I heard young women of the Conspiracy office complain bitterly about spending hours typing (and often writing) speeches for the defendants, with no acclaim accruing to them (and no pay either). According to one woman, Rennie Davis—scorning their

complaints—had advised them that they "should be grateful to
do anything you can to help the men of the revolution," a bit of
arrogance which I, even as a nonfeminist, found contemptible.
Having been involved in the work of organizing, I could not
personally complain of having done nothing but type or make
coffee for Movement causes . . . but one thing that happened at
the march filled me with impotent rage. It was rage that had
been waiting a long time to erupt, I guess, but even now I can't
regard the incident that catalyzed it as silly or trivial or irrelevant: Abby Hoffman goosed me—simple as that. The day of the
march—the culmination of long months of work—was marrow-
chilling damp; I had been up since 6:00 A.M., and standing on
the platform I experienced waves of the buoyancy (which feels
like ecstasy) that comes with great physical weariness and emotional release. Pete Seeger was singing *Give Peace a Chance*, and
Abby Hoffman, gratuitously and for the fun of it, came along
and goosed me. At another time I might have regarded it as a
clownish prank. That day—I think out of the lucidity of physical
exhaustion—I thought, He despises women . . . and the women
had all worked so well, so hard. That relatively unimportant
incident was the proverbial "straw"; as much as anything else it
predisposed me to accept Mimi's invitation to attend a Sex-roles
Committee meeting. After I decided to attend, I began to think a
lot about my sweet, complicated children—strong, gentle-tem-
pered, introspective Josh, and fragile, fierce, assertive, vulnerable
Anna—about their choices and their options. When I came to my
first meeting, I felt, quite remarkably, absolutely at home—as if I
had been a feminist all along.

We were indeed disparate and diverse. And we were obviously,
at this point, a long way from defining our goals and grievances,
and even further removed from a course of action that would
establish us as partners of the staff, and not as antagonists.

    Almost immediately the group incurred some hostility because
of its decision not to invite fathers to early meetings. (Indeed,
one of the first questions I had asked was, *Men are invited too,
aren't they?* I thought that if sex-role stereotyping was a problem
at all, it was theirs as much as ours. I was as concerned about my

son's happiness as I was about my daughter's, and I didn't see
how we could accomplish anything without fathers.) Committee members still continue to dispute the correctness of this decision. Two women summarize the conflicting points of view: one
woman who initially protested the exclusion of men reversed her
thinking and said her earlier stance had been "naive and wrong.
They'd have been distracting and threatening. We would have
spent too much of our time taking care of them. We had enough
problems raising our own consciousness and trying to formulate
our own approach to the staff." Another active committeewoman
is convinced we made a mistake in failing to involve men more at
the beginning. Her contention is that some women might have
worked within the group if they had felt their husbands were
involved. "They were not strong enough to do it alone, and they
felt, quite rightly, that it was as much their husbands' concern as
their own. Those women were lost to us, and we've never really
gotten their participation." She argues that our decision made it
appear almost as if we were punishing women who had good
marriages.

The corollary to this was the charge—which the Sex-roles
Committee challenged but never quite succeeded in overcoming
—that we were an "elitist" group because we were selective in
our invitations. Carol London, who has a daughter in the eighth
grade, remembers being "resentful and angry when at first nobody asked me to come to sex-roles meetings. I thought the
committee was a lower-school clique. I wondered how people got
in. I couldn't figure out how you decided whom to invite." My
own feeling is that initially, the women were about as sloppy as
they were enthusiastic; there were no organized mailings, and all
invitations were word-of-mouth, so naturally we invited women
we felt for some reason would be sympathetic. I distinctly remember one sex-roles committeewoman hanging around the
school's corridors waiting for teachers to pop out of a classroom so
that she could invite them to meetings. There was plenty of zeal,
and we did announce meetings in the school newsletter, but still
some people persisted in feeling that the committee was a closed,
cliquish in-group.

During the early fall months, sex-roles committeewomen were speaking to the administration and to individual members of the staff, soliciting their involvement in our concerns. We tried—not always successfully—to convince our friends and acquaintances on the staff that we were not motivated by hostility, that we were indeed grateful that our children had this oasis of kindness and caring, but that we believed that with parents and staff working together, a very good thing could be made very much better. (That's what we said. Often the reason we couldn't convince the staff that it was also what we meant was that our attitude did, in fact, tend to be condemnatory: *How could you have deceived us by allowing us to believe our children were happy here?* Like all converts, we felt we had been duped.) What we said was: "Just as black parents are asking you to examine your attitudes in relation to black people, we are asking you to explore your attitudes about sex roles. And just as black parents are asking Woodward to take another look at its curriculum, its readers, and its library books with the nonwhite children in mind, we are asking that the curriculum, the readers, and the library books be reexamined with girls in mind. We were not always tactful, and not always prepared for the inevitable defensiveness of people and institutions asked to question the basic premises of their conduct. Woodward likes to consider itself innovative and avantgarde, which indeed it is; but the snag was that, in this case, parents, not staff, had initiated the process of questioning and reevaluation. It was also natural, perhaps, for teachers and administrators, tired of hearing the anecdotes offered as evidence that Woodward was sexist, to feel threatened by the ardor of militant feminists. Meanwhile the sex-roles committeewomen perceived that they were being treated like an outside pressure group, and they resented it. It seemed as though every time a feminist began to enunciate complaints she was stopped dead in her tracks by the question: "But what do you *want?*" never an easy question at best, and since in this case we were merely beginning to formulate what we wanted in concrete terms, it was a very disconcerting one. The Sex-roles Committee was, at least at its inception, regarded as an adversary group.

Individual discussions with teachers on a person-to-person

basis were often fruitful, and each committee meeting gave us more clarity of purpose, but this was not sufficient. Sex-roles committeewomen were eager to involve the staff on a formal basis. We wanted, first of all, to get Ruth Fishman and Gertrude Goldstein to come to meetings. This may partly have been because we were beginning to feel that we were talking into a vacuum; but we also knew that there had to be an open committee–staff discussion before we could understand how to form a working relationship with the staff. When, in early November, Gertrude was asked to attend a Sex-roles Committee meeting, her first question was: "How many parents have you got?" What she was really asking, of course, was, *Am I dealing with a few crazies, a splinter group, or is there a broad base for this thing?* We convinced her that we would have thirty families represented at the meeting, and surprised ourselves by having more than forty.

Gertrude and Ruth came to that first really large meeting with mixed feelings. It was no longer easy for them to believe that they were dealing with the gripes of a few eccentrics. They immediately objected to the fact that only women were invited. Gertrude said later that at the time she felt we were dealing with family situations that could only be solved if men and women worked together, while now she sees that involving men can't be the first step in radical feminist activity.

I too now agree that the decision not to invite men to early meetings was the correct one. Women who are just beginning to find their own voices and their own identities, who are exploring new ways of seeing and being, wish to do so in the company of other struggling women. When we begin to will ourselves to see ourselves as autonomous creatures, we must do so without men, who have traditionally assumed the role of protectors, mentors, and judges.

I think it is true that if we had invited men to early meetings we would all have been watching the men's reactions, as it were, out of the corners of our eyes; their presence would have been distracting.

Gertrude admits to having felt defensive at the first meeting she attended: "I had always considered myself a feminist. Here I was—I'd been a professional all my life—and these young snips

were acting like they'd discovered America. I was jealous of
them. After all, I'd spent half my life asking myself, Am I castrat-
ing? Am I feminine enough? They were able to feel they could
have a husband and kids *and* a career. I had to keep wondering
if my success was threatening to my husband. I felt I had to
'make it up to him' for being a professional woman. I didn't think
they'd understood my struggle. It's hard to be a woman director,
they don't know . . ." Gertrude, whose frankness has charmed
and disarmed many parents who were prepared to do battle with
her, admitted that as a professional woman, she was afraid of
alienating men, and she also felt superior to other women. "It took
me a long time," she said, "to realize how boring men can be—
before that I had thought only housewives were boring—with
their talk about cars, war, and how to get from here to there; at
one professional meeting I heard a man talk for fifteen minutes
on alternate routes to the George Washington Bridge! But I had
accomplished everything alone, without a Movement, and now,
suddenly, leadership was coming from the parents. I felt
pounded. I felt like you were pointing an accusing finger. You
provoked guilt, and we felt threatened. My inclination was to
say, 'Don't tell me what to do; you've created the situation in your
own homes.' "

At that meeting—which most of us, in retrospect, see as the
beginning of the real impact we were to make on the school—
various personal styles that were to continue to mark the group
began to emerge: there were the smoother-overs, the confronters,
and the on-the-other-handers. Also, it seemed to many people
that a dichotomy of perceptions—an ideological struggle we
were to thrash out over and over again, and one which has
continued to confound the women's Movement as well—was becoming painfully obvious. While some women seemed to value
everything male above everything female, taking the line that if
men were work-oriented, competitive, and perceived their world
analytically, it behooved women to be and do the same, there
were others who celebrated the typical female modality. Sensitivity, compassion, nurturing, conversation, and lack of aggression were seen by these women as proof that women were, in fact,
superior to aggressive, competitive men. Some women, for example, bemoaned the fact that, while men seemed happy to talk in

abstractions, women were more comfortable when talk gravitated to personal relationships. Others saw this as a source of strength, a proof of greater sensitivity and superior moral virtue. The gap between the two groups was sometimes very wide indeed. Some women expressed bitter resentment at not being respected—at, rather, being jeered at and caricatured for the arduous and significant domestic and community services they performed—while others felt that domestic functions by their very nature were despicable and sterile, whether or not they were remunerated, since both paid domestic and volunteer laborers were powerless to impose their will on the world. Some women saw their oppression as being primarily sexual and psychological; others, who felt a strong obligation to make their personal struggles relevant to those of working-class women, saw it as having derived from a capitalist society.

The magic word that served to unite everybody—and we all breathed a sigh of relief when it was mentioned, because it reduced debate to manageable proportions—was *options*. We had to keep reminding one another that the essential nature of our struggle at Woodward was to provide our children with the option to become whatever their singular natures led them to choose to become, regardless of prevalent stereotypes. This concept had a lovely, workable simplicity that succeeded in deflecting the which-is-better quarrels, although—since no one but a fool or a saint can value all things equally—differences of perception and ideology kept flaring up.

Gertrude Goldstein, Ruth Fishman, and two lower-school teachers came to this first large meeting. Three black women came to the meeting as well. Some sex-roles committeewomen were exhilarated by the meeting—which they perceived as exploratory, and as such, a satisfactory beginning—while others remember both the staff and the black women as sources of tension. One woman said in retrospect, "People were too careful of staff members. I remember trying to explain a specific instance of sexism on the part of a male teacher, and another sex-roles woman immediately smoothed it over as if Gertrude and Ruth would be alarmed, or frightened away."

(I'm not sure it's an irony, but it is certainly interesting to note that women whose politics were radical often came on more gently with the staff than women whose politics fell roughly into the liberal category. Adrienne Yurick remarked to me, "The school isn't an Enemy Institution, General Motors is an Enemy Institution. Defensiveness built up on both sides once we began to see individuals and the staff as villains, or The Others.")

The topic for this meeting was *Perceived Differences Between Boys and Girls . . . Are Girls Less Intellectual Than Boys?* It had been carefully chosen by the women who organized the meeting so as not to suggest an attack on the staff, and so as to cultivate the idea that we were engaged in a mutual exploratory process. Actually, the meeting turned out to be more interesting for the questions it raised than for those it answered.

When we bemoan the fact that girls see clouds as pretty and boys comment on how they "work," aren't we attaching more value to the male orientation than to the female, we wondered; aren't aesthetics as important as mechanics? Why devalue the girls' contribution? Aren't both perceptions valid? In any case, weren't the boys expressing, not their intellectual curiosity, but their knowledge? Then we questioned why, if both perceptions were indeed valid, the reactions remained stereotypical. Why did all the boys react one way and all the girls another, unless they had been programmed to think in those stereotypical ways? This led to the question of whether, when we comment on a girl's pretty dress, or pretty hairstyle, by "rewarding" her, we are in effect forcing her to "think pretty," and to draw her satisfaction from "pretty"?

Six-, seven-, and eight-year-old boys are more exuberant and physically aggressive than girls, we agreed, which led us to ask how intimidated girls are by this. In organized wrestling—a teacher-directed activity—boys play to win, while girls are concerned about alienating their friends. We asked whether this cliquishness of girls, their desire for popularity, and their changing alliances, were not another form of aggression, a manipulative and punitive technique that hurts in the same way that boys' physical aggressiveness is designed to hurt. When a girl becomes identified as a "tomboy" and shares in boys' activities, is she not then more respected, by both boys and girls? Aren't exuberance and aggression, therefore, highly valued by a child's peers? Shouldn't we be as concerned with the suffering of a boy who is not physically aggressive, who cannot live up to the superhero image, as we are with the intimidation of girls? Are we willing to say that we prefer the girls' verbal aggression to the boys' upfront body language?

There was discussion as to whether or not we were ignoring class or racial differences. Were we ignoring developmental stages and age differences? Hadn't it been our experience that daughters who were pretty-frilly-ornamental one year often became book-oriented, independent, exploring, and physical the next? Our daughters acquire academic skills earlier than our sons, but then, around puberty, they achieve less, while boys achieve commensurately more. *How did we account for this?* How could we change it? How could we look at our children in a continuum?

If we actively encouraged girls to do "boy" things—pretend to be astronauts, or wrestle no-holds-barred—and directed them to mechanical rather than to aesthetic appreciations, didn't we run the risk of squashing the essence of the child? How much could a teacher push a boy to an easel, for example, or to sew a patch-work quilt, without interfering with his freedom of choice? On the other hand, we wondered if we could in fact, speak of "choice" when children eight or nine years of age have already gotten the message that only certain options are available, and that these options are based on gender. Wasn't it more a matter of "squeezing back in" than of squashing out?

Many of these questions had already been raised at earlier sex-roles meetings, but it was to keep happening that questions explored and resolved among the core group of feminists would be reexamined as new members joined the group, so that numerical growth—in terms of furthering action and analysis—was also perceived as stagnation. Strains between staff and committee, and between white and black women, were already apparent at this meeting, and were later to become exacerbated, while the question of men's involvement with the group was again to become a focal point for dispute and contention.

At the close of the meeting, Ms. Goldstein requested that we become part of the PTA, and she offered the group a parent-staff liaison teacher, Maia Scherrer. Although PTA jokes rank second only to mother-in-law jokes in the repertoire of stand-up comics (the very mention of either is usually good for an automatic laugh; having thrust our roles upon us, men are always eager to caricature them), Ms. Scherrer's appointment and the group's becoming an ad-hoc committee of the PTA were important symbolic acts: they served notice that we were—although perhaps still regarded warily—an acknowledged, legitimized committee working within the school establishment. One of the sex-roles committeewomen reports that when, at an earlier PTA meeting, she suggested that the PTA members become involved in the Sex-roles Committee, she had been greeted with "sniffling, snorting, and tittering." (It would have been unthinkable, of course, for anyone to sniffle, snort, or titter at the Black Studies Committee at that time; that was taken as evidence of the relative strength of the two groups and the seriousness—or lack of it—with which we were taken.) Still, one or two women in the group, although they might have been expected to enjoy having the last laugh, vehemently opposed being absorbed into the PTA, behaving in a way that implied that this relatively powerless group was at least as malevolent as the CIA. Their fear was that we would be "co-opted." The majority of the committeewomen felt, however, that joining the PTA was merely a formality (as indeed it proved to be), and that we would lose nothing by joining the PTA and perhaps gain broader acceptance as well as a forum. So we agreed. In retrospect, the debate as to whether or not to join seems to have been a hassle over nothing at all.

Spurred on by the good feelings engendered at this meeting (for although some thought staff members had struck a defensive attitude and had sometimes been less than forthright, most of us were encouraged), the sex-roles group embarked on an undertaking that proved to be ill-advised, and very nearly disastrous.

The Black Studies group provided the inspiration. They had had sensitivity-training sessions with the staff, had presented the staff with curriculum materials (and demanded that they be used), and were always—in one way or another—confronting the staff successfully, or so it seemed to us. We wanted to make our presence felt as they had. We thought that the lesson to be learned from the black parents was that the school responded positively to pressure. So we asked Ms. Goldstein to assemble the entire staff so that representatives of the Sex-roles Committee could meet with them and "talk things over." It was a very bad mistake.

One woman remembers going to that meeting in her "lady disguise"; she says she was so eager to make a good impression, she wore a dress for the first time in months.

Andrea Ostrum says: "We came to the meeting with enthusiasm, but no real plan. We thought we'd talk about 'feelings.' They said, 'What are your goals? Where are your educational materials?' while we were trying to talk about attitudes toward girls and boys, and about teachers' expectations. We retold all the anecdotes—hammers and nails and blocks and dolls—and I could feel their resistance. We were disorganized," she acknowledged, "and I think the staff used that as an excuse for not listening, for not dealing with content. Then we got nervous and anxious when they didn't respond, and we became accusatory. We panicked."

Another committeewoman, Adrienne Yurick, points out, "The staff really wasn't ready for us. Their consciousness wasn't raised about sexism the way it was about racism. The first part of the meeting was uncomfortable and desultory. Then we started making demands, but there was no feeling of exploring together . . . working together . . . it fell apart."

Gertrude Goldstein's memory of this confrontation is that it was "attack/defense. You're bad/we're good." "When they started giving examples and telling stories, I said, Oy! That story again! How come when I'm not God-the-Mother people are outraged? Why didn't we get credit for the small Japanese woman who taught woodwork? How come we didn't get credit for a male teacher cooking with the boys? How come all we heard about was what we were doing wrong?"

Maia Scherrer also remembers the ill-fated meeting: "You were so hot with an idea. You were crusaders. You were going to right the wrong in two minutes."

Pushed against the wall of the staff's resistance, the feminists said they wanted access to classrooms and curriculum. They wanted sexist books removed from the library.

The staff was outraged. They responded heatedly:

"Our classrooms are open. Don't you monitor our classrooms."

"We're the professionals. We'll see to the curriculum."

"What curriculum materials do you have to give us?" (We had none.)

Maia said, "Hitler burned books."

Worst of all, some staff members—we had thought we were a long way beyond this by then—said, "Who's discriminating against girls?"

We had been guilty of bad timing, and of a failure of imagination. As the sex-roles group dispersed, discouraged and dispirited, we felt that we had hardened the staff against us, and that we had established ourselves as adversaries.

# 4

# Winter 1970: Changes

There, little girl, don't read
You're fond of your books, I know
But Brother might mope
If he had no hope
Of getting ahead of you.
It's dull for a boy who cannot lead
There, little girl, don't read.

—ANON.

If a boy acts up, I make him sit among
the girls. They hate that, they do.
If one's really naughty, I make him,
sometimes her, sit on the floor. But
mostly we have a rare old time.

—MRS. SARAH DRAKE,
Schoolteacher, Southall, England.
(New York **Times**, March 28, 1972.)

The Sex-roles Committee, by now disabused of any notion that change at Woodward would be effected quickly and painlessly, continued to meet. Our discussions, which before had tended to deal with concepts such as intellectuality and aggression and how they were manifested in boys and in girls, began now to center on our relationship with the staff. It had been brought home to us that we were perceived as critics, not partners—and insensitive, bullying critics at that. We tried to get more teachers to attend meetings, but even this was seen as bullying. While we felt particularly sensitive to the charge of being an elitist group and were trying to rectify this by opening up our meetings, some

staff members perceived our aggressive solicitation of their attendance as negative pressure. Sex-roles committeewomen began to
weary of talk. We knew that we needed to recoup our losses after
the staff-meeting fiasco, and we knew that educators love materials. We knew also that we still had a large reservoir of goodwill
to draw on among teachers and administrators, and among as yet
uninvolved parents.

So in January, 1971, after the children returned from Christmas vacation, the committee invited the Feminists on Children's
Media—a collective of mothers, high-school students, librarians,
and professionals in writing, publishing, and education—to present a slide-and-talk program at a general meeting of the PTA.
All parents and staff were invited. At that meeting—in a sense
our "coming out" party—hundreds of illustrations from children's
books were projected, in all of which girls were depicted as
dependent, passive, beribboned, ruffled, playing "little-mother"
housekeeping roles, or playing wide-eyed little sisters to boys
who were physical, dominant, intellectually aggressive, and
courageously in control of their world. The evidence was massive
and incontrovertible: a girl's world is narrow; she must take delight in small, homely pleasures. A boy glories in pushing against
constrictions, leaping over boundaries, thrusting himself against
his ever-widening world.

The collective has, apparently, made little impact on the
Brooklyn Public Library. On a recent visit to the main branch, I
saw a display shelf labeled BOOKS FOR GIRLS. I counted ten books
that fell roughly into the category of "dating and romance"—one
of which had to do with the terrors of acne—six that had airline
stewardesses as heroines, eight that featured nurses, several that
extolled the glories of ballet dancing, four in which "tomboy"
heroines—imaginative, spunky, adventurous and funny-looking,
girls—blossomed out of braces into sweet, passive, pink-pedestal
femininity before it was *Too Late*. Naturally, no self-respecting
boy would read any of these books, and since there was no
corresponding shelf labeled BOOKS FOR BOYS, presumably boys
could choose from the whole wide world. No boy would fall for
the implication that ironing daddy's hanky is as much fun as
chasing frogs or rainbows. The male contempt for females and
femaleness is bred early. There's nothing contemptible in ironing

daddy's hanky, but why should girls see an act such as this as not only the zenith of pleasure, but the only sanctioned pleasure, and a female obligation, to boot?

It was clear from the collective's presentation that when girls developed physical and intellectual confidence, assertiveness, and strength, they suffered a corresponding loss of "femininity." And that, while male characters worried about *what* they would be, female characters worried about who *he* would be. Needless, perhaps, to say, there were no books about gentle, nurturing boys, although there were some about "sissies," who were converted—of course—to *macho* malehood. Yet there can be no question that the male stoic superboy image is just as damaging to boys as the female stereotype is to girls. Firstly, it allows them to think of girls as soft-sillies, teaching them to require weakness of girls and then to despise them for it. Secondly, it places upon them the burden of always having to be strong, never dependent, or needy. (My small son, for instance, watching a television adventure film, once said, "Look at the silly ladies. They're always scared and fainting." Then he added, "Mommy, does there always have to be a man catching the silly ladies? Doesn't a man ever get scared and faint?")

The collective's evidence of the inexorable channeling of boys and girls into their ordained roles was virtually irrefutable. Not all staff members were present, but those who were, were enthusiastic, as were the parents. No one really tried to deny the evidence that girls were instructed to be docile, passive, nonassertive, and dependent, while boys were offered role models that were independent, resourceful, active, and assertive. There was, however, some discussion of mothering and housewivery as opposed to "work." A few women protested that mothering and nurturing were gratifying, honorable vocations. *Nobody had said they weren't.* Most feminists present expressed their feeling that these were, indeed, humane and gratifying activities, but that they were not the only vocations open to women, and not every woman's inescapable destiny. We stressed again that we were talking about options, and deploring the fact that a girl's life is so circumscribed that her choices frequently go unexamined all her life; other people—her husband, her children—become her "job" without her ever asking herself if she has a place and a "work" in the world outside her domestic domain. We never did succeed in convincing many women that we were not suggesting we pop all our kids into day-care centers and all run out and get nine-to-five jobs. I suppose the reason for this was that, for some of us at least, feminism had become an inspiration for planning to return to school, or to return to jobs in the outside world. We were on fire with newfound commitment to the selves that had previously languished in kitchens. If a vote had been taken among Woodward's feminists *at that time* it would probably have demonstrated that most of us did see housework and volunteer work as unattractive, unrewarding jobs. So our talk about options was, to some extent, disingenuous. Many of us did see nine-to-five jobs as the path to salvation, and some of us probably did—as zealots will—harbor some contempt for women whose temperament led them to choose and value traditional modes of being. It is easy to overglorify and romanticize "work," particularly if you're a young, white, middle-class housewife and have never been faced with the onerous necessity of toiling at unpleasant jobs to earn a living. For many feminists, work outside the home is the first step away from impotence and isolation and toward self-realization, but it can make them insensitive to the fact that for many other women, work outside the home is just a multiplication of drudgery. I think that many Woodward feminists eventually moved away from their intransigent (though inarticulated) positions about the superiority of work outside the home (which offered them the appealing vision of money and power for which "self-fulfillment" can be a euphemism). Most of us now see the issue for the complicated one it is, and understand that *work* and the exercise of *power* have infinite gradations of good and bad. Much has been written about the powerlessness of women, and some feminist writers seem to feel that any power—even the power to exploit others—is better than none. But I think most of us at Woodward would reject the power, say, to run things at ITT, or to enforce the will of United Fruit on banana republics; in other words, we do not aspire to exercise power in a ruthless, manipulative way, or an exploitive way. That is not because we are "pathologically afraid" of power, but because we would reject the power to do evil. Most of us would probably agree that if a feminist revolution is to succeed in making all of us truly human, we have to redefine success—which means redefining the importance of the symbolism of money, and redefining power— and not in the terms that a male society has set down for us. In any case, most of us do not now view careers as a panacea. Feminists who would rather bake birthday cakes than litigate corporate law don't feel obliged to apologize. Many Woodward feminists share roles with their husbands; both partners work part-time and spend half their time looking after the house and children. We are all beginning to find individual solutions to our problems and needs regardless of gender, which was—of course —the point all along. One sex-roles committeewoman (the mother of two young children), told me recently that she returned to her consciousness-raising group after summer vacation and announced, sure of a hostile reception, "What would you say if I told you I was pregnant?" To her surprise, she shocked no one. A year ago, she said, she would have shocked everyone, including herself, because everyone was feeling the pressure to "do her own thing," and one's "own thing" was not thought to be compatible with having babies. *Her* own thing, she had decided, was to be primarily—for the time being, at least—a housewife and mother. Certainly motherhood is a true vocation for some women and affords them more gratification than any career might. But it is not *every* woman's true vocation, nor does it preclude the necessity for other gratifications. Men don't have to make this either/or choice that they—and sometimes, unfortunately, spokeswomen for the women's Movement—have sought to force upon women. What we must strive toward for our daughters as well as for our sons is that they choose roles out of strength and in harmony with their own revealed natures, not passively allow themselves to be assigned roles that are antithetical to their true needs.

Our attitude toward work was undoubtedly simplistic, at the time of which I'm writing, which was understandable in the context of our blind acquiescence in the roles assigned us. We were experiencing the sheep-led-to-the-slaughter bitterness and resentment of people who feel that they have not participated in their own fate. Our talk about options was often less than heart-felt; it gave black women, whose attitudes about work had been forged in a very different crucible from ours, the right to wonder what we had in common with them, just as it justified the plaint we heard from one house- and community-oriented traditional woman, *You're condemning everything I do!*

At the time of the Feminist Collective meeting, however, these nuances went largely unexplored. The meeting itself was judged by all to have been a great success. Bibliographies of nonsexist books were distributed, and orders were taken for books that had been carefully selected both for their story appeal and for the unstereotypical way in which they delineated boys and girls, and men and women. New parents expressed interest in coming to sex-roles meetings. Best of all, the meeting had served to "legitimize" us as a group. The rancorous hangover from the staff meeting had been largely dissipated. We had gained respectability.

Consciousness-raising at sex-roles meetings, individual discussions with staff members, and the Feminist Collective meeting all started to bear fruit: we began to see changes at the school. The staff committed itself to reevaluating its library and its readers and to ordering nonsexist books. The physical setup of nursery and kindergarten classrooms, which had encouraged grouping according to sex, was rearranged to facilitate the movement of children without regard to boy/girl definitions. Ms. Goldstein began to encourage fathers to perform some of the exacting and time-consuming tasks that had previously fallen only to women. "Class mothers" were thus transmogrified into "grade parents," about a third of whom are now men. Class lists were revised so that the names of both parents were listed. Several fathers found themselves momentarily at a loss for words when their grade chairperson telephoned to ask if they would contribute a casserole to the school bazaar. Previously, when a Woodward mother telephoned to speak to a parent on a school matter, a father's automatic response had been, "Just a minute, I'll call my wife." We weren't inundated with manmade casseroles, but we felt that by not allowing men to assume automatically that this was their wives' job, we had raised their consciousness.

The increasing participation of fathers in the life of the school had been given impetus by an article in Woodward's March 1971 newsletter—the newsletter, a parent cooperative venture, became a forum for discussions of sexism and racism—by Bob Ubell, husband of a sex-roles committeewoman.

Consider this situation, which . . . actually happened at Woodward: Two first-graders—a boy and a girl—are playing doctor and nurse. The girl, whose parents happen both to be physicians, plays the role of the nurse, and the boy is the doctor. The teacher asks the little girl why she doesn't take the part of the doctor. Without batting an eye, the girl says, "But girls aren't doctors!"

Obviously, the little first-grader has been well trained. This despite the overwhelming evidence in her own home denying the pat response. Surprising? Not very. Consider this: fathers of Woodward children know that the Parents' Association is a women's organization, else it would not be so apparently dominated by mothers. And the women oblige their husbands by filling all the posts and taking on many of the tasks as their exclusive domain. The fathers are delighted and I suspect don't even feel a twinge of remorse at their abdication of responsibility. After all, it is women's work. When pressed, Woodward fathers must admit that the education of their children is a joint responsibility . . . but it's much more convenient to leave the routine chores to mommy.

Since our children get their signals—their modes of behavior—from the adult world, whose intricate mysteries children try desperately to unravel, no wonder they respond at ages four and five as if they had taken an intensive course in male chauvinism. Every overt or subconscious act we perform, whether it's racist, sexist, or plain nasty, is just another clue for our children as to the kind of behavior which we will accept as proper from them.

Naturally, the clues that Woodward fathers give their children about the school would lead them to believe either that the whole business is so boring that it's not worth any of father's time, or that the child's education is just another dim star in the galaxy of mother's chores. . . . [In] the [typical] suburban family . . . the father's car is always the brand new American model and the mother's is always the beat-up foreign job. How can mother be so important? How can the activities with which she is involved be so valuable?

I don't think it's fair to expect the school alone to care for the education of our children, nor is it sane to continue to expect the mothers to carry the responsibilities of the Parents' Association. Of course the ladies are doing a good job. Don't they always?

(American men often complain that mothers have too great a role in the lives of their children, and that they exert too much influence, dominance, and smothering power. But, because it's true, as Bob Ubell says, that everything mothers do is made (by the same men who complain of the overprotective, domineering mothers) to seem despicable or trivial, men grow up hating, fearing, and despising women. They have contempt for them as insignificant creatures at the same time as they blame them for having controlled and molded their lives. In fact, men who feel that feminist "interference" in their children's education is just a way to gain more power over their children need to be reminded that if women have power to control their own lives, their need to live through others and to control the lives of other less powerful human beings is reduced.)

Pressure, persuasion, and the justness of our cause had produced changes; but these were only token victories. We were concerned about a climate. We had made little impact on the curriculum. So far, we had concentrated our efforts on the lower school, and we were not sure how to reach the many teachers we felt were still resistant.

# 5

# Consciousness-raising or Political Activity?

> Every emancipation is a restoration
> of the human world and of human
> relationships to man himself.
> —MARX

We knew that we—or the women's Movement—had made a real
connection with several teachers, whose new feminist awareness
had changed their classroom ambience. By this time, several
teachers had joined their own consciousness-raising groups. Others were still hostile to us or to feminism; some were defensive,
while some professed indifference or disdain. Sex-roles people
were of two minds as to how to deal with the staff and as to how
to effect profound and pervasive change. Some committeewomen
thought we could not create the nonsexist attitudes we wanted,
or change the curriculum to reflect these attitudes unless we
broke down defenses and reached through to underlying feelings. They felt that unless staff members had a feminist consciousness, and unless we raised the consciousness of many more
parents for a wider base of support, change would be impossible.
These people wanted to win more hearts and souls over to the
cause. They wanted more consciousness-raising meetings, and
they fretted when staff and parents did not eagerly accept eagerly proffered invitations. Other more action-oriented sex-roles
committeewomen were particularly concerned about having an
immediate and direct effect on the curriculum and on educational policy; where they saw sexism practiced, they wanted to

intercede and demand change. These women were preoccupied with the practicalities and mechanics of ways in which the curriculum might be enriched, and encouraging role models for girls introduced. The question, then, was whether to consciousness-raise or to engage in political activity. What we were actually engaged in was a hassle over a variant of the troubling question: can morality be legislated? For several late-winter and early-spring months we spent more time quagmired in the consciousness-raising versus political-activity debate than we did perfecting a program to implement change. There were debates within debates: for example, in the name of political activity a few women pushed for structured—as opposed to leaderless, free-wheeling—"sensitivity" sessions with the staff. There were women within the group who wanted to make use of various psychotherapeutic tools and devices to get the committee and the staff to "communicate" and "relate." This idea, the notion of working on interpersonal dynamics rather than stressing concepts, content, or analysis, drove a lot of other people up walls. The Black Studies group had not only provided the staff with curriculum materials, it had also engaged the staff in sensitivity-training sessions. They seemed to us a much more "together" group than we were, and sometimes our invidious comparisons with them made us despair.

The problem was exacerbated by the shifting nature of meeting attendance. Sometimes as many as forty people—staff and parents—met in a parent's home; sometimes as few as eight. A small nucleus always came. Staff attendance was erratic. Perhaps ten teachers came, at one time or another, most of them women, and most, teachers in the lower grades. Committed feminists were often impatient at having to "start all over again" at every meeting. Trying to get it together with a group of people at every conceivable level of consciousness is like trying to have a formal conversation with people at various levels of sobriety, or like generals and privates working together to plot a battle campaign. Moreover, we had no hierarchy; we were leaderless. I remember reflecting that if Mussolini had believed in participatory democracy, he might have gotten the trains to run on time, but it would have taken him a lot longer. No doubt there would have been a couple of engineers who would have argued that there was something inherently abhorrent about trains that arrive on schedule, and—however quixotic it might seem—the proponents of this belief would have had to be permitted to express—and vote— their conscience. Anyone who has ever been to an open political meeting, particularly anybody who has been involved in radical, or Movement, politics, knows how hard it is to get anything done (the sole exception being *Who's going to take the minutes?* Since there are always fewer women than men at political meet- ings, and since it's assumed that a woman will always take notes, the field is narrowed by better than half and that problem gets resolved with dispatch). We were no exception.

Often our militance got in the way of our sensitivity, and we were consequently guilty of failure of imagination and lack of empathy. For instance, we were often impatient when new peo- ple brought up issues that we had already resolved to our own satisfaction. Of course someone who is reading Dostoevsky doesn't want to diddle around with people who are still learning the alphabet, but we did bad (rash, impolitic, and unkind) things. I remember one meeting at which we were discussing tactics: a woman who had not been to meetings before said— and it was obviously heartfelt, coming out of bewilderment, if not anguish—"But I don't want my son to be a *mother.* What if he turns out to be homosexual?" A sex-roles committeewoman hushed her up, whispering urgently, "I'll talk to you about that later." Well, it's true that we'd had that one over and over again, but *she* hadn't. She took the rejection as a slap in the face, as well she might, and she never came back. Another time, a very deter- mined feminist inveighed against television, delivering herself of the opinion that no self-respecting feminist would allow her chil- dren to watch it at all. Several women felt that the circumstances of their lives could not permit them to take such "pure" positions, and they were intimidated, turned off, and angry. We often, not out of malice, but in our anxiety to *get on with it,* failed to deal with people's fears, and with the fragile egos of women who felt less radical than the articulate, verbally aggressive feminists in the group. We sometimes set stern standards that not every- body could, or wanted to, meet. People like to be liked and to feel comfortable. They like to feel that attention is being paid to them, and we didn't always make it possible for them to feel that way.

I asked several sex-roles committeewomen to look back on that time, and these were their comments, from which it is apparent that even in retrospect, unanimity on tactics was never achieved. It's also apparent that no one perceived what actually happened in the same way as anyone else.

Adrienne Yurick, whose political convictions are coherent and cohesive, maintains that "the school was defensive; but it's in the nature of institutions to defend themselves against change. It was a mistake for people to personalize, to see individuals as villains or the school as an enemy." Having worked with many groups, she contends that "It's true that there had been no previous pattern of people working together with the staff in the way we were attempting to do. But when the staff said *OK, we know we have a problem, now what do you want us to do?* we should have developed ways of exploring together. We might have worked harder to form a co-committee for problems and techniques of change. We might have found ways of coming to mutual decisions. We got angry and took power positions. We should have had more consciousness-raising sessions. I'm sure it looked to them as though we felt *we* did everything right and *they* were ruining our kids. Although we felt an urgent need for a relevant curriculum, they didn't want us to presume to teach. I think what we needed was mutual involvement with the curriculum, with ultimate responsibility in the hands of teachers." Adrienne agrees that the extemporaneous nature of the curriculum added to our difficulties, and she puts her finger on an essential truth: "When women experience a leap into feminist belief, they tend to have contempt for people who are not where they're at. We hold others responsible for what we did before our conversion."

Vivian Ubell, who always expressed concern for the more "traditional" women, and resisted judging anyone by how "feminist" she was, feels that people who were not in the "advance guard" felt left out. "There were not enough outspoken moderates. I don't know why women with stronger consciousness couldn't have made it more comfortable for people with less awareness. I think what happened was that we had to prove that we were *real* feminists; people felt pushed to articulate stronger and more radical positions than they actually held. It froze people out who were still in an exploratory stage. It's true we invited everybody,

but only a small core of us defined group goals. Divergence was
really not welcomed. We didn't talk about boys enough, for instance; there was just a perfunctory response to the sufferings of
boys. And in general the committee put a down-trip on good
teachers for minor infractions. The initial resistance would have
been there whatever we did. Then we zoomed in on what they
considered petty, and I think our criticisms were too acute
and too narrowly focused. It wasn't fair to dump on the staff for
not having conceptualized ideologies when they really were trying to see each child as an individual." Vivian shares Adrienne's
feeling that "we needed more consciousness-raising, both among
staff members and among parents."

Peggy Sandback, who finds it impossible to outshout anybody,
and who is acutely sensitive to people's reactions, says, "It was
hard for us, locked into our own individual perceptions, to talk
about what we were struggling with personally. I got paranoid; I
felt that the relationship with the school was so ambiguous.
Sometimes when we talked about what was happening at school
I felt that I was telling secrets." Discreet and scrupulous to a
fault, Peggy says, "I never knew how freely to talk about teachers. The whole thing evoked childhood guilts; it was like telling
on your best friend. I could never figure out whether our loyalties
were to the school, to the kids, to one another, or to issues. I can't
see even benign authorities as 'friends,' and my feeling that we
might be maligning teachers and that it might get back to them
was really oppressive, but we never dealt with feelings like that.
I'm not saying we should have done group therapy; but maybe
we should have been more patient with one another and willing
to go over the same ground more often for people who needed
that kind of support."

Andrea Ostrum was decidedly and rigorously "action-oriented.
I favored direct approaches to the school. I don't think we proceeded badly at all, except for the initial staff meeting." Andrea,
whose manner is as patient as her convictions are steely, does not
share the belief that we did not engage in enough consciousness-
raising: "As far as I was concerned, our goal was to change the
school; consciousness-raising among the parents was secondary.
It was counterproductive for new people to come in all the time.
I felt that the group had to consolidate."

Donna Barkman believes that what we did is exactly what most of us would encourage other groups to do now; we consciousness-raised, and—when it was appropriate—engaged in direct-impact actions: "Although we got bogged down many times in the either/or controversy," she says, pleased with the way we comported ourselves, "I always felt we had to work on all levels at once, and that we were, in fact, working on both levels at once. To establish relationships between people and clarify ideas is as important as action. Those people who wanted to do concrete things—to provide material, for example, or to complain about blatant cases of sexism—did so. I personally saw the two things as interrelated. Materials aren't going to do any good without consciousness-raising; on the other hand, if the staff wanted materials and was more comfortable with them than with abstract talk, then materials were important. They were one way to raise their consciousness. In fact we were doing both things all along, and I don't know why we had to argue about it so much."

At the very time that some committeewomen were flagellating themselves for being "elitist," Gertrude Goldstein was feeling that "attendance was pounded and forced. There seemed to be an equation of honesty of purpose with attendance at meetings. I felt a partial commitment from the first meeting I attended, but during the spring, when I guess it was felt that change wasn't taking place fast enough, I felt a lot of anger coming from the group." To which Ruth Fishman adds, "Yes, but that anger, when it was expressed, broke down categories and barriers. I think the evolution of the group was natural, and I felt there had to be opposition of will for us to move together."

The contrasting points of view of two staff members intimately involved with this group at this time are also interesting:

"I really hadn't thought at all about 'women's things,'" said Meg Bluhm, a third- and fourth-grade teacher. "If you hadn't invited me, I probably never would have given it much thought. I found the meetings searching and exploratory. I didn't feel the need to be defensive. I didn't feel that I had to pretend I was perfect, because the parents were examining their own conduct as well as the staff's. I never felt any conflict about the legitimacy or the validity of what the group was saying. Almost immediately, I found my own consciousness-raising group outside the school." She added, "I haven't been at Woodward long. I guess if you have, you have to defend the 'honor of the school.' I wasn't there long enough to be defensive. I loved the first meeting I went to, and I didn't feel attacked. I thought people were understanding and kind."

Maia Scherrer's reflections about the discussions she heard then, on the other hand, are not positive. Maia is one of the kindest people I know. I have seen her engage in acts of astonishing generosity, for which she exacts no gratitude. She is also very determined and forthright; she respects people who struggle—a "coper" herself, she is impatient with "whiners." "I blame middle-class women for the fix they put themselves in . . . they had options. People can transcend their circumstances. I get impatient when privileged women sleep all morning and then whine about their lives. I hold individuals responsible for what their lives have become." Maia also felt a tendency on the part of the group to value male things over female things, and to romanticize men's lives. "I think it's important to ask whether we are trying to ape men or really to fulfill ourselves," she said. "I sometimes had the feeling that women were horrified when girls liked to play with dolls, or liked babies, but I think we can warp our daughters by putting down childbirth. After all, Life is what it's all about, isn't it? We fight against the war because it damages life, so how can we hate childbirth? I've always believed that it's possible to be a whole person with or without marriage, and with or without children. Yet sometimes it seemed that Movement women were condemning every woman—including humanistic, contributing citizens—who had no jobs and earned no money."

Unquestionably, women did often articulate fierce positions. Perhaps they felt, initially, that they couldn't control their own damaged lives, and so they worked with more determination than subtlety through their daughters. It's also true that a certain amount of "whining" went on. But, just as the assumption of extreme positions was necessary, at first, for many women, to enable them to redress a psychic imbalance, the "whining"—the insistence on shared pain—was a necessary step before they changed their lives. Few of them sleep all morning now—and in any case, I think it's possible to sympathize with people who sleep all morning (who are victims of "housewives' depression"), when their sleep-hiding is interpreted as a pathological exhibition of deep, unselfinterpreted malaise. I don't agree with Maia that middle-class women are gifted with options. I suspect that part of her feeling that this is so stems from her deep empathy with working-class women with whom she has worked for much of her professional life. Privilege is not the same as options. Options exist only if one can see the possibility of reaching out and grabbing them. They do not fall into one's lap like ripe plums. Furthermore, women's "reach" and vision have been so thwarted and narrowly focused that we don't see and can't reach for the plums because of the forest of false assumptions we live in. I do agree, on the other hand, that some people are able to transcend their circumstances if they're brave, or lucky enough, and that we all have ultimately to take responsibility for our own lives. It is to be hoped that consciousness-raising groups will go beyond the sharing of pain (and I admit that sometimes feminists act as if pain were a banquet to be enjoyed forever) and take that responsibility. I don't think it's quite fair to demand of women who have been so crippled by their socialization, and who have been taught what to feel as well as what to think, that they cast away their crutches without some preliminary wailing. As for Maia's contention that we were "condemning" traditional women (she had in mind women who did civic- and volunteer- as well as housework), I think it's fair to say that these women have long been acceptable to our culture. They have in fact, been offered as the "norm," and considered "natural" women. Women who derive gratification from this role feel comfortable in it because they are rewarded by society with the knowledge that they are doing what they are supposed to be doing. They are not the freaks of our society. Who speaks for the women who are *not* gratified by traditional roles? In the past, they felt like freaks . . . they were considered unnatural women. What the rhetoric— however heavy-handed—of the Movement has done is to enable nontraditional women, women with unstereotypical aspirations, or women who couldn't delight in their assigned roles not to feel like freaks. It is a little unrealistic to ask newly liberated women

to defend the role of the traditional woman. She has already had
her share of defenders and eulogizers. Perhaps we might have
said "on the other hand" more, but having seen the other side of
the question for so long we were rather tired of looking at it.

It's difficult to know whether Maia's objections sprang from
the fact that we didn't do enough consciousness-raising, or from
the fact that we did do too much general, directionless rapping,
and that it palled; or whether she would have felt the same in
any case. It is interesting to note that although she was the staff-
committee liaison person she never verbalized these feelings at
meetings, and neither did anyone else, although she must surely
not have been alone in thinking as she did. I think Maia's silence
within the group was symptomatic. Objections like hers were not
fully explored; there was no forum for them. It's almost impossible to say whether the reluctance of good, caring people like
Maia to talk about some of their more negative feelings toward
the group could have been erased if we had used some other
"technique." I think we were scrupulous in our self-examination.
I've seldom been in a group that questioned its motives more
vigorously. Yet, while we felt responsible for everything that
happened or failed to happen at Woodward, it's important to
remember that neither we nor the school were acting in a vacuum. The women's Movement had gained media exposure and
currency, and we were all responding to external events as well
as to one another, and also bringing to all our meetings the
baggage of our own internal, personal struggles. At least part of
what we said at meetings was probably a kind of testing, talking-
aloud means of dealing with the changes in our own lives. The
terms of many marriages were being reexamined; women were
making difficult career decisions and political choices—it was a
time of flux. Staff members acted and responded both as individuals and as an institution, while sex-roles committeewomen acted
and responded as individuals, and as a group. Whether we could
have drawn more people to us if we had structured things differently is impossible to say. The alacrity with which some people
responded to us probably had less to do with us than with the
fact that they themselves were ready for feminist ideas and politics. That others did not respond to us probably had less to do
with what we were doing "wrong" than with the fact that they

were just not ready for what we had to say. We could have been perfect, and still obtained less than 100 percent support. We were far less than perfect, yet despite differences in style and ideology, despite frequent failures of communication, we worked together functionally and we accomplished radical changes.

The issue of whether to consciousness-raise or to engage in political activity resolved itself—though not to everyone's satisfaction —in mid-spring.

We decided to provide the staff with the educational materials they seemed to crave, or at least to demand when we pressed our needs. We broke into work-groups to research papers for presentation to the staff in June, at the end of the school year. Our approach was more eclectic than scholarly. We each did what appealed to us. One group of women committed itself to preparing materials (including video tape) on sexism in the media, focusing particularly on children's television programming and advertising; several women formed a committee to present research papers on women in history, the image of women in literature, and a paper on psychological testing—particularly tests indicating gender-based differences in modes of perception and cognition.

In the meantime, as subcommittees formed work-groups for the presentation/workshop, sex-roles meetings continued to be forums for consciousness-raising among parents. What we were doing—even as we proceeded with seemingly endless talk—was very much in the spirit of the articulated pattern of Women's Liberation consciousness-raising groups: we consciousness-raised, and simultaneously with our attempts at refining a feminist analysis, we engaged in direct immediate action where it seemed appropriate.

# 6

## Black and White

> If colored men get their rights, and
> not colored women theirs, you see the
> colored men will be masters over the
> women, and it will be just as bad as
> it was before. . . . Consider on that,
> chil'In.
>
> —SOJOURNER TRUTH

> Tonight we will argue and shout,
> "My loss is greater than yours,
> My pain is more valuable!"
>
> —ANNE SEXTON

When black women attended Sex-roles Committee meetings,
those meetings were occasions for bewilderment, acrimony,
anger, and pain. We wanted a feeling of solidarity with black
women, both because it was an emotional necessity for us, and
because we deemed it a tactical necessity to present a united
front to the school. But the differences between black women
and white women were so profound that goodwill, kindness, and
intelligence were not always enough to bring us together.

The Black Studies group at Woodward is determined to in-
crease the number of black teachers, and to see to it that the
curriculum, the library, and all materials reflect the black experience. It is developing a skills-resource bank among black parents,
so that parents with specific skills or interests may share them
with the children, thus providing positive role models. Black parents want their children to understand the history of oppression,
and to learn about slaves and suffering; they also want their

children to learn about the artists and teachers and scientists—
men and women, strugglers and liberators—who were not beaten
down by oppression, but who, amazingly and with grace and
fortitude, transcended the horror of their imposed situation.

The Sex-roles Committee at Woodward largely parallels these
aims. It is determined to see to it that the curriculum, the library,
and all materials reflect the experience of women; it is developing a skills-resource bank among women, so that women with
specific skills or interests may share them with the children, thus
providing positive role models. Feminists want their children to
learn the history of women's oppression, and to understand the
societal and cultural limitations that have been imposed on their
lives; they also want their children to learn about the artists and
teachers and scientists—the female strugglers and liberators—
who were not beaten down by oppression, but who, amazingly
and with grace and fortitude, transcended the horror of their
imposed situation.

In the school newsletter, Marge Hammock, a black parent, set
forth what she wanted for her black children:

> Bob Teague says in the opening of his book, *Letters to a Black
> Boy*, that all black folks are insane. The insanity is, of course,
> attributable to the daily and unrelenting confrontation known as
> racism—all kinds of racism—racism that lets people starve and
> live in terrible housing, racism that deprives folk of dignity,
> racism that creates a thousand Newarks, Atticas and Birming-
> hams. The slave system is alive and well, and flourishing in this
> world.
>
> The most insane thing about it is that many of us black folk
> work, sleep, eat, try to raise families, laugh, talk, get mad, cry,
> and manage to go on being alive and constantly looking for some
> way out—some alternative to madness.
>
> Those few of us over thirty who have managed to become
> "credentialized," that is, skilled, semiskilled, college-trained,
> middle-class-value-oriented, have in a way become more insane
> than some of our so-called less fortunate brothers whose life-style
> (determined primarily by money) has not changed.
>
> Many will remember being told that the only way to get rid
> of the *poverty* life-style was to:

   *1. Be clean and moral and uphold the law of the land.*
   *2. Work hard and imitate white role-models.*
   *3. Speak "proper English" and be polite.*
   *4. Disassociate oneself from "common" Negroes.*
   *5. Integrate at all cost.*

Imagine what happened to some of us when, in the early sixties, young students broke the law and gained concessions, and seamstresses and ministers formed coalitions that led to boycotts and national movements.

Some of us did find out for the first time that it was possible to be angry and insane and not die immediately. Further, we found out that it was possible to maintain a black life-style and not be cut off from all those goodies that we said we must want. And then in the seventies many of us had to admit that integration was painful and in many instances not even desirable.

All of this is to say that it is hard for me to clearly identify what I want for my children in this crazy world. . . .

It is most important to point out, especially to those under thirty, that our elders did, in some oblique way, manage to convey to us some other things besides being clean; even though we did a lot more whispering than wearing black-power buttons, and even though we did wish for security, status, and beauty of the *Good Housekeeping* kind, still, many meaningful things that I want for my kids came from my now-ninety-year-old grandmother. In many ways, her input is as strong for me now as that of Malcolm X, Ron Dellums, Melvin Van Peebles, and Angela Davis.

   1. I would want my children to have a good feeling about themselves as black people and to know that they are a part of an enormous family and community in America, the Caribbean, South America, and, of course, Africa.

   2. I would want them to know that black people have always had a life-style based on sharing and community and that we are reexamining our values so that they reflect this older life-style and a basic love and responsibility for other black people.

   3. I want my children to know that they have a proud heritage; I want them to have a strong need to find out as much as possible about that heritage so that they will not have to be dependent on anyone outside their community for information about themselves.

   4. I want my children to know that black people have been brutally victimized and are still being subjected to calculated cruelty.

5. I want my children to know that there is little that black people can expect from white institutions, but that it is vital to keep making demands in order to guarantee primary survival, while creating those institutions which are responsive to the needs of black people.

6. I would hope that my children would understand that racism is a way of life for many people, and that being the victim of racism has nothing to do with one's competence as a human being.

7. I want them to understand that, as their mother, I wish their beauty, curiosity and warmth to take them where it may, but that at times I must interrupt the flow of that curiosity and warmth to explain, for example, the horrible, painful reasons for Martin Luther King's death, so that they will be prepared to cope with the pain ahead of them.

8. I want my girls to develop strong antennae for put-downs, stupidity, and arrogance, and to learn *all* of the options for dealing with the threats to their dignity.

9. I want them to have all of the basic skills necessary for survival and nation-building. Their interest in scholarship and excellence should be motivated only by their own personal drives and the needs of their community.

10. I want them to know that being free has nothing to do with being indifferent to the feelings and needs of others, and that responding warmly and directly to those around them has nothing to do with archaic protocol and court behavior.

11. I want them to know everything about this total society and how it functions, so that they can understand what has happened to all people and why they must concern themselves with making positive changes.

Finally, I want them, through knowledge, sensitivity, and honesty, to be able to cry for all the black sisters doomed to feeling "ugly," and cry for all the black men and women doomed to feeling helpless. I want them to be able to understand all the black people who try to escape the pain of their blackness. I want them to understand their rage, when it comes, and make it a positive force.

I hope that they will never lose their ability to laugh, love, and share some of those beautiful things that happen to black people when they are together, and, out of all that sorrow, rage, and love, be prepared to take part in that great black change that I hope may one day become a reality.

Most of Woodward's black families are middle-class. They tend to value traditional academic skills and traditional educational methods more highly than do many white parents. They also tend to be more "formal" than many white parents. Barbara Mask told me, "You know, black people react negatively to the informality of whites. When a white family invites a black kid over, there's usually some suspicion. Some people can't help wondering, *Do they want our kids for their token integration factor?* Then, when they see what goes on in white houses—like kids running around practically naked, and using 'language'—it's easy for them to think, They're acting that way because they don't respect black people and they don't care what they do around us. Well, I don't know if that's paranoia or rigidity. Naturally we have a chip on our shoulders. You go crazy, being black. All black people are a little crazy."

The black women I spoke with varied in their attitudes toward the school and the way in which it was dealing with racism:

Barbara felt that the school was generally responsive to black parents. "I think their caring is genuine," she said. "It's unrealistic to think Woodward's ever going to be a black liberation school. I don't want it to be an all-black school. My kids aren't going to live in an all-black world. Woodward can't give my kids a really good black identity, no matter how much black studies materials it provides. But I can do that at home." I pointed to my son's long-lasting, best-friend relationship with a black child at school and asked Barbara if her observations confirmed my feeling that relationships between black and white kids at Woodward were genuinely healthy. She said, "I see healthy, loving relationships between black and white kids at school. But then I wonder, Can my kids afford to have the white friends they have? It won't last, that's what makes me sad. There are going to be inevitable differences of direction, they're going to have to assert their black identities . . . and when they start dating, that'll be the end of that."

Marjorie Hammock (who intimidated me when I first met her, because I misread her reserve and initial cautious approach for coldness) feels that "it's significant that the school keeps referring to us as the *Black Parents* group, as if what we were trying to do was going to benefit only black kids. The truth is that the total school benefits from understanding the black struggle. We're not a special interest group; what we're doing has universal value. Understanding the black liberation movement leads to all kids really looking to themselves as agents for change." Marge surprised me by saying she'd be happy to see some ethnic studies at Woodward: "Hell, they take the kids to Pennsylvania to visit the Pennsylvania Dutch—the Hasidim are just down the street; why can't they visit them? What I mean is, the school isn't a melting pot—why should it be? I'd like to see them not try to cover up differences—I mean biological differences, differences in food, music, life-styles, dress—and make sure that all the kids know that variety is good and healthy. I know a white teacher who wouldn't let her long hair down because she said the black kids made too much of it. What she should have done was said, Yeah, my long straight hair is beautiful—and so is yours. She could have strengthened the positive images. She could have looked at the hair of a black kid and the hair of a white kid under a microscope, for example. The trouble is, they're oversensitive, sometimes, to what we might think, so they don't do things like that. They're just not comfortable with us." "Why?" I asked. "We scare the shit out of them, to tell the truth," Marge said. "There was one teacher who said she felt uncomfortable dealing with slavery because the white kids felt guilty. Well, that's too bad; sorry about that. It's her job to help kids with their feelings. She has got to figure out a way to deal with it, that's all." Marge does not feel Woodward ought to congratulate itself for having black studies: "Big deal. The black culture pervades everything, we're not so special. When I hear President Nixon talk about the 'nitty gritty,' I know it's all over . . . maybe we'll have to talk in a foreign tongue if he's going to take over our language. Yoruba for me."

Terry Babb, another parent active in the Black Studies group, felt that "Gertrude and Ruth were more responsive to black needs than any other administrators would be. Still," she said, "we keep providing them with materials—film-strips, records, audiovisual stuff—and they say they don't want to 'lay it on the kids,' they want stuff to come from the kids, not from 'materials.' So a lot of the stuff we give them ends up on the shelves. I get the feeling we're being pacified. Maybe this isn't an argument about racism, maybe it's an argument about educational approach. When I'm feeling really cynical," she said, "I think . . . the staff's chief aim is to protect the school; the survival of that school is what's important. They'll do all kinds of juggling acts to keep it alive . . . give a little to this group, a little to that . . . just so long as the institution survives. That's the real commitment."

There is some irony in the fact that, while white sex-roles committeewomen were having the Black Studies group urged upon them as an example of a disciplined approach to the organization of study materials, and perceived the black group as a model of political effectiveness, most black parents felt that the materials with which they had provided the school were not being fully utilized.

Sex-roles committeewomen admired the black parents for their united approach to the staff. It never occurred to us (we saw them as a firmly knit group that spoke with one voice on philosophy, tactics, and goals) that they might be having the same kinds of internal struggles as we were. In fact we held them in some awe (although one black woman told me that our attitude was "just a fancy way of thinking all niggers look alike. Where are your heads at, don't you think we're human and have differences too?").

Terry Babb exclaimed: "We argued all the time within our own group. We thought *you* were together. We looked to you like we had it together; that's because you don't really *look* at us. Half the time we're invisible. . . ." You've got to understand: never mind this nonsense about the black woman walking two steps behind the black man. It's side by side, baby, or nobody walks at all. . . . Right, I won't argue with a black man in public." Terry sensed that I thought she contradicted herself. "Understand," she said, "I'm not doing it to preserve his ego, but to have unity in the black family. You know I'm not going to let him get away with bullshit, but I'll tell him out in the hall, not in front of white people.

*What are we going to do about the black women?* Again and again, sex-roles committeewomen voiced this cry. We wanted very much to feel that black women were part of the group, and

I think we sought their participation for several reasons, or combinations of reasons, none of which was "pure."

Many of us had what we believed to be true and good friendships with black women, and we wanted to share our new awarenesses with them. As a group, we were committed to the idea of sisterhood and we wanted genuinely to reach out. Since each of us had learned to see ourselves reflected in other women, we assumed that working together would prove what in our hearts we already felt to be true: that what we shared in common, our femaleness, was of greater significance than those things (racial) which might be pulling us apart.

One can interpret this attitude as innocence born of ardor, or one can acknowledge that our naiveté stemmed from the fact that most white women at Woodward had never (regarding pleasantness as a virtue and as a cause for self-congratulation) directly confronted the black women they were eager to claim as sisters with the basic questions: *How do you feel about white women? What do you think we feel about you? How does color affect sex roles?* The black women would say, of course, that we had never directly confronted our own racism. One may also argue that there are times when innocence is a luxury and an indulgence one cannot permit oneself.

We were keenly aware of the fact that we—and the women's Movement in general—were vulnerable to the criticism of being a white, middle-class movement. We needed the black women, therefore, to assuage our guilt and to disarm our critics. We knew that the broader our support, the more likely we would be to get what we wanted at Woodward; to put it bluntly, we knew that it was good tactics to involve black women in the struggle.

Consequently, individual sex-roles committeewomen had been inviting black women to attend sex-roles meetings all along, but their response had been less than gratifying. They seldom attended, and when they did, they distanced themselves from us—physically, by sitting outside the "circle," and emotionally, by saying *you*, when the rest of us said *we*, and by coming late.

While we were busy seeing them as The Black Women (a block), they were busy seeing us as Them (a block).

Of course, responses and perceptions varied from person to person. For example, there was one militant black woman who affected sex-roles women particularly strongly: "She comes on like God in a tractor," one woman said, while the reaction of another was that "she's absolutely incoherent with pain." The first woman became prickly and withdrawn every time this black woman showed up, while the second became syrupy and over-solicitous.

Some women tended to bend all their encounters to fit into a preconceived political construct; others had psychological formulations and categories which they applied to every human exchange. To operate exclusively out of either a political or psychological bag is, of course, constricting and banal. People who "psyched" everything out, and people who had ready-made political rhetoric, had "magic words" to interpret every variety of human behavior: words like "politically correct" (or "incorrect"), "hostile" "judgmental" (or "nonjudgmental"). Magic words, fetishistically invoked, seldom are susceptible to vigorous analysis. They also serve as a buffer, or insulator, protecting their users from open and vulnerable, intuitive, or visceral response, and they arrest the flow of compassionate or empathetic responses. Few of us can make an imaginative leap into another person's consciousness—or into another person's skin—and most women (black and white) tended merely firmly to plant other women squarely into their own frames of reference. (I include myself, of course.) This is not to put down either the Sex-roles Committee or the black women: we all have our totems and crutches. The amazing thing is not that we seldom achieved true empathy, but that occasionally—as individuals, not as groups—we transcended our own self-imposed limitations, and *did* achieve it.

*What to do about the black women* became an even more urgent and pointed question in late spring of 1971 as we prepared our papers for presentation to the staff in June. Our papers and the subsequent workshop-discussions we had planned were to focus on three areas: history, literature, and the cultural and societal stereotyping of women and female children as exhibited in the media. Would it be *white* women in history, *white* women in literature, and *white* women in the media, or would we include black women as well? We had hoped that black women would work with us on our projects, but this did not happen. Would the white women, then, research the black experience themselves? When the women preparing the history paper suggested that they speak to the organic relationship between the suffrage movement and the abolition movement, several women countered with "magic words": we can't presume to speak for black women. The rationale for this politically "pure" position was, I suppose, that the experience and heritage of white women would necessarily lead them to sources and perceptions antithetical to those of black women. The women who determinedly espoused this point of view defended it by analogy: just as men can't speak for women because they're insensitive to the issues and unmotivated, not having been in women's place . . .

There is some justification for feeling that this attitude is politically incoherent, and self-conscious, and perhaps self-righteous. Barbara Mask, exasperated, commented: "For goodness sakes, anybody who can read well and is reasonably intelligent can do a research paper." I think it is true that one can dig out sources and point to facts without *interpreting* the black experience. One way of looking at it was that, by saying "we can't presume to speak for black women" we *were* being presumptuous, because we made the assumption (without asking them) that the black women would find it offensive for us to do so. As it turned out, when the black women learned that we had decided to deal only with the white experience, *that* offended them. It was all a muddle, and it took several black-white meetings, in which tensions finally exploded, to bring it to a resolution.

A meeting was called so that the women preparing papers could make a progress report and read preliminary versions of their papers. One of the sex-roles committeewomen had extended a special invitation to a black woman to—as the black woman remembers it—"speak about black women from my perspective." The trouble was, no one besides the woman who had extended the invitation knew that the black woman had been specifically invited. The conversation washed around her. It was, as all sex-roles meetings were, informal and leaderless. Used to more structured meetings, the black woman felt ill at ease, interpreting even the formlessness of the meeting as a direct affront to her, and one calculated to keep her in her place. She still talks about that meeting with urgent pain:

Although she impresses most people as being completely,

coolly in control of her emotions, she says, "I get uptight when I try to talk about race and class. I'd been specially invited, but I felt like I was skipped over when everybody was talking. I began to feel uncomfortable. You know when you're being ignored, and I was being ignored. I felt horrible. I'd done a lot of homework. I felt invisible—like I was supposed to be the maid. Why didn't anyone ask me why I wasn't speaking? Why didn't the woman who invited me help me? I felt like I was just being tolerated. I don't know what kind of hostesses you are, but I know when I'm chairing a meeting, I'm conscious of silence, and I invite and elicit response and opinion. That's what people do when they're really concerned for other people. Nobody at that meeting did that for me. It got late—after eleven—and I was furious; I knew I was either going to cry or scream . . . or kill. Well, I yelled: I said, I've been in this room for three hours and I've been systematically ignored. You're afraid to confront me and you're afraid to confront your own racism. The meeting broke up after that. Like, I'd dropped a bomb, and everybody was shocked. The next day I got a lot of phone calls; you whites were upset, all right. But I didn't feel like putting myself through that again."

The white woman who had extended the invitation says: "She distanced herself. But it's true that I treated her as if she were invisible. I'd invited her personally. I felt a special responsibility I couldn't deal with. I guess I expected her to make her own way. The truth is, I'm afraid of black women. I think their style is one of cultivated toughness. It intimidates me. I can deal with it honestly in a one-to-one relationship, but not in groups. That meeting was awful. I felt responsible for hurting another human being."

One of the women who was working on the history paper says that she had wanted to include black women in her paper— "after all, if women are more or less absent in history books, black women are nonexistent"—but that she'd allowed herself to be intimidated by the feminists who were adamant that black women had to speak for themselves: "I didn't really know how that was going to work," she says; "they seldom came to meetings, and when they did, they didn't express themselves. But I didn't want to antagonize them. I wanted the black women to like me." She recalls the pre-presentation meeting at which the papers-in-progress were read, as a "nightmare. I hadn't dealt with black oppression in my paper at all, and as I read it, I could feel the tension in the room. I was sweating—literally. I could tell that the black women were angry—which was just what I'd been trying to avoid—and I felt fear and dread. I'd planned to ask them for their perceptions and additions afterward, but I couldn't even do that. I know that it must have looked like I had total disregard for black women, but I just didn't know how to deal with any of it."

Nor, it seemed, did anyone else. Everyone in that room was aware of tension, but no one "named" it—everyone acted as if it did not exist—until finally, toward the end of the meeting, a black woman said, "I'm very, very, very angry; nobody's paid any attention to me or to relationships between Third World women and white women." The woman who'd read the history paper, who was close to tears by then, says she wanted to lash out: "I wanted to ask her why she thought she should get special treatment. Her silence wasn't our fault. Why should the burden have been on me and on all the white women to try to interpret the feelings of the black women?" This woman felt "dumped on," and resentful of the fact that "other white women went overboard to protect the black women's feelings. I hadn't known that the black woman who blew up had been specially invited; how was I supposed to know? I thought her anger was manipulative. Everybody was intimidated by everyone else. She felt ignored, and she shouted at us. But we weren't able to say how we were feeling. We were all walking on eggs. Nobody was relating in a human way. The white women seemed to consider it their obligation to accept anger without expressing any. . . . I resent anybody who makes me feel guilty."

Several weeks later the committee met again to discuss the presentation to the school. By this time the antagonism between black and white women was more or less out in the open. A black woman, in a rather rambling statement to the group, managed to say several things that outraged the white women: she said she was resentful of the fact that Women's Liberation was a "media fad" and resentful that it had taken attention away from the black liberation struggle because it was "flashy and chic"; that what she'd heard about the women's Movement was largely irrelevant to her because black women want to "get out of other folks' kitchens and into their own," and therefore talk of careers did not reflect their concerns; and she said that if black women or white women went on the job market in force, it would take jobs away from black men.

The white women were visibly upset. I remember reflecting (silently) that women who allow their men to support them have been cursed for spoiled indolence and exploitation; women who rebel against being supported and protected are now cursed for competing with men. Whatever we do is wrong. And it did not seem fair to me to blame the inequities of a capitalist society on the needs of individual women who are impelled, or obliged, to put themselves on the job market. On the other hand, if "jobs," careers, nine-to-fives, are what the women's Movement is basically about, then of course a black woman who identifies with her working-class sisters has a right to wonder what relevance the Movement has for her. If Women's Liberation is narrowly interpreted as a rebellion against housework, then of course it may be seen as having relevance only to the middle-class. But the rebellion against housework (which, it is true, gave the Movement much of its impetus) is really a rebellion against a state of affairs that decrees woman to be a creature of relative importance, whose identity is to be found only in serving the superior creature, man. When women began to question why it was appropriate to speak of a "working wife" or a "working mother" when it would have been absurd to refer to a "working husband" or a "working father," they began to understand that they were—regardless of their position in life—part of a servant class; their rebellion was a rebellion of vassals who chose to escape—not merely the kitchen, but the prison of definitions imposed upon them by others. What feminists say is that each human being must have a work in the world—must be free to find his or her own calling—regardless of gender. (It is, unfortunately, true that the middle-class bias of many Liberationists leads to the assumption that any woman who liberates herself by getting a job is likely to get one that's either fun or prestigious or both, as befits her superior intellect and education, an assumption that overlooks the fact that work for the working class is, generally speaking, no fun at all. As one woman remarked caustically to me, "Those ladies ought to try working in 'Chock Full o' Nuts' for a while.") Many feminists would like to see traditional "women's work" given the prestige and accorded the respect they think it merits. For these women it is significant that, although we are told by male critics that there is nothing more important than rearing the young, our society—a cash-nexus society—in fact rewards women engaged in traditional occupations by paying them the lowest wages on the scale. We are all—career women as well as housewives—penalized for being women. Our society pays lip service to traditional, "natural," women, yet pays domestics, housekeepers, baby-sitters, and nursery-school teachers lower wages than those paid to bartenders. Needless to say it pays mothers—those pillars of the republic—nothing at all. In a society where work is rewarded with cash, the dollars are not being put where the eulogies are, and black women suffer from this duplicity at least as much as white women do. It's hard to escape the conclusion that women are despised regardless of what they choose to do.

Furthermore, many of the white women at that meeting, they later reported, understood from what the black woman was saying that they were being asked to postpone the satisfaction of their own needs until black men achieved theirs. Naturally it is painful to be cast in the role of oppressor (in this case, as exploiters of unemployed black men) when one has just begun to understand, oneself, that one belongs to an oppressed group. It is like some grotesque game of musical chairs in which someone newly aware of her own victimization suddenly becomes pegged as a victimizer. Many of us who initially saw the feminist struggle as essentially (and simplistically) one of oppressed females against the male oppressor have had to endeavor to expand our political consciousness to allow our imaginations to encompass the oppression of others—even when the oppressed others may appear to be our oppressor. (A revolution achieved at the expense of others who are also oppressed is not the kind of revolution most of us would wish to live or die for.) The charges the black women made struck a sensitive nerve, because many of us were beginning to deal with considerations of class and race that we had hitherto not fully explored. It takes great seriousness of purpose—it is very hard work—to translate visceral feminist feelings into a political analysis that takes into account all of the evidence. While many of the white women were grappling with a political analysis, most of us felt struck in the viscera. Our reaction was a deadly combination of unspoken anger and paralyzing guilt.

The charge that the media has seen fit to take up Women's Liberation is justified, of course, though to see a newsman who isn't either amused by feminists, or condescending, or vitriolic, is rare indeed. Earnest though the media may feel obliged to be about everyone else's struggles, newsmen tend to make little jibes at us; they keep us as pets.

The white women, who were dealing with a plethora of feelings—all of them uncomfortable—did not allow themselves to be verbally upset. We were reacting both to the substance of the charges (which we were trying to sort out), and to our feeling that we were being unjustly accused of never having considered the relationship of black women to feminism. The undeniable fact that *we* had not brought these issues out in the open ourselves added to our discomfort. Our silence seemed to intimate that we accepted condemnation. (At least two people told me that they went home that night and threw dishes around the kitchen to give vent to the pent-up frustration that came with not being able to "slug it out.")

Open animosity—or frankness, depending on how one saw it (and I cannot see it dispassionately, because I was a participant in this scuffle)—broke out, when the paper on "the image of women in literature" (which I was preparing) was discussed. After I read the paper, a white woman said to me, "Why didn't you include black women?" My response was that I had not felt free to deal with black writers, and that, having written the paper with several themes in mind, I had chosen books I knew well, which were illustrative of the points I wished to make. I said something like, "All my life, I've been in other people's movements. This Movement is about *me*. When I prepared this paper, I wrote what I knew. Of course if a black woman wants to

add her own perceptions, I'd be glad." The white woman who
had raised the objection interjected: "Racism is a priority," to
which I remember replying, "I'm my first priority for the first
time in my life. It's the first time my feelings haven't been located
around the pain of others. I'm addressing myself to *my own*
oppression; for one thing, it's the only one I can talk sense about.
. . . I've been in the civil rights movement, and it was horrible . . .
because I found myself speaking for other people's needs, not
my own."

Thinking this exchange over in retrospect, wondering whether
I would retract any of it now, I find that I was speaking simplistically and with more fervor than accuracy. My response was a
visceral one. It was also an innocent one—and I mean innocent
as a pejorative; innocence is often offensive. To interpret the
personal experience one has had in social movements requires a
certain amount of political sophistication, which I lacked. I
would certainly not attempt to deny my personal experience—
which was that, for me, working with black men in the civil-
rights movements had been a discouraging and painful experience. (I felt, as did many women I knew, oppressed by the
chauvinism of black men. White women who had sexual relationships with black men were put down: "She's in the Movement
because she's looking for a stud"; while white women who did
*not* have sexual relationships with black men were also put
down, and told "You're really a racist underneath because you
won't go to bed with me." A classic case of "damned if you do
and damned if you don't." I'm not trying to imply that this is a
problem peculiar to black males. The truth is that most men—
black or white—have contempt for the women they use casually;
and most men—black or white—will use any ruse, any guilt-
provoking argument to get a woman into bed with them. Nevertheless, I have a certain amount of sympathy for women like a
friend of mine—who did in fact spend quite a lot of time in
Southern jails—who remarks bitterly that "it's a little hard to
take, when you're ready to go to jail for your principles, to be
told that you're really a racist underneath.") I still believe that
the only firm ground to stand on is that of one's own necessity.
However, it now seems clear to me that the personal is always
political; that personal experience cannot be understood in a po-

litical vacuum. Marge Hammock, for example, when I talked
with her about my experiences in the civil-rights movement, said,
"What you don't understand is that the civil-rights movement
was not only destined to fail, it was *designed* to fail. Black people
didn't know who they were, and white people didn't know who
they wanted black people to be. White people thought they had
to love everybody, and when they didn't get loved back, they
hated." If Marge's comments had been explored by the Woodward group, black and white, it would have taken experience out
of the personal and into the realm of the political. But we seldom, as a group, were able to do this. It was difficult, in a group
situation, for us all to make ourselves vulnerable to one another
and to talk about painful feelings freely. There must be a way to
start from one's own necessity, but not to allow one's necessities
to blind one to the necessities of others. Finding that way—
finding a way to communal endeavor without sacrificing personal
truths—is what makes any revolutionary undertaking so im-
mensely difficult, and what made it so hard for black women and
white women to work together at Woodward.


Meanwhile, at the meeting, Andrea Ostrum, who had prepared a
paper on psychological testing, and gender-based differences in
perception, spoke to us about the fact that, in tests of spatial
ability, boys perceive analytically, in terms of parts and whole,
while girls consistently see things more globally, in terms of their
entirety; they are more likely to be influenced by all the elements
in the field together. Translated into practical terms, this means
that boys are likely to keep trying various solutions to problems
until one works. Global thinking is not the kind of thinking most
conducive to high-level intellectual productivity, especially in science or math. Children who are analytic, as opposed to global,
are more likely to be independent and self-assertive . . . boys,
therefore, are likely to be more independent and self-assertive
than girls.

  This analysis led to an argument. Some women were eager to
establish the fact that no psychological test is "culture-free" since
the bias of the tester (male) is likely to interfere with the results.
These women were, in effect, denying that there were gender-

based differences in perception; they saw the tests themselves as basically oppressive to girls. Other women accepted the tests, and deplored the results: why, they asked, were girls so disadvantaged, and how can we change the training that so ill-equips them to think analytically? A third group of women resisted the idea that analytic thinking was necessarily better than global thinking, arguing that to contend that women have been cheated by not being programmed to think analytically meant that we valued the male mode of perception over the female. (It's easy to say, sanely, after the fact and the imbroglio of discussion, that neither mode is despicable, but that what is deplorable is that *most* boys think one way and *most* girls think another, revealing that even the tools we use to understand ourselves and the world are not freely chosen.)

It turned out that most of us in the room that night felt inept at dealing with figures. In the general discussion of global and analytic thinking that followed (in an atmosphere already tense because of the aborted discussion of whether or not racism was our priority), one of the white women mentioned, without investing the remark with much significance, that when she was in the supermarket she couldn't "figure out whether to buy two cans for 55 cents or one for 26 cents."

A black woman snapped at her: "If all you had to spend was 45 cents, you wouldn't have that problem." The implication was, of course, that the white woman who couldn't manage supermarket prices was a spoiled, privileged person who would have managed to learn if she had been faced with economic necessity. Trying to smooth things over, the white woman (who later complained, "Nothing I could say could possibly move that black woman—she was determined not to recognize any of my problems because I'm middle-class—*she's* middle-class too, that's the irony, and three cents makes as little difference to her as it does to me") did what people usually do in circumstances like these: she dug herself in deeper and made things worse. "What I mean," she said, "is that if my cookbook says to cook a roast for twenty minutes a pound and the roast is three and three-quarter pounds, I have a big problem."

Whereupon the black woman said, "If you knew your old man was going to be home at six o'clock and he'd wipe you out if the dinner wasn't cooked, you'd figure it out." To put this in perspective, it's interesting to note that the black woman who attacked—no doubt out of her own feeling of despair that the white women were not dealing with class questions—was certainly not married to a man who would "wipe her out" if she didn't get the dinner on the table on time. What's true also, of course, is that poor and working-class women are the chief victims of consumer frauds, rip-offs, and supermarket pricing. Necessity may be a good teacher, but desperation often obscures the point of the lesson. The battering exchange in question might have led to a fruitful discussion, but it didn't. It didn't because we were all nourishing our own pain, we were all defensive and bruised, and we did not, therefore, address ourselves to the political and ideological questions implicit in the charges leveled at a middle-class white woman by a black woman who, though also middle-class, identified strongly with working-class women. Our feelings got in the way of real political discussion; conversely, the fact that we were all at different places politically tended to abort frank expression of our feelings.

I asked several women to look back at that time, and this is what they have to say:

One white woman said:

"The black women came to meetings and remained separate, and we made little effort to include them. We were all self-conscious; it was unnerving. I remember one black woman saying, 'You are disorganized; you are not militant enough.' She told us how we should be pressuring the school. But she didn't consider herself one of us. Why was she scolding us? Jesus, how can you talk to anyone who's yelling at you all the time? Every time a black woman started ripping into us for being middle-class I felt wiped out. Like they were telling me I wasn't entitled to my pain." This woman says that after consciousness-raising in her own women's group she felt "stronger and less muddled and entitled to my own pain—it's *my* pain, after all, and *my* suffering —and I don't feel I have to apologize for it. I did feel guilty and apologetic then, though, like, What right do I have to suffer?"

Another white woman feels that the major problem was that

the white women never dealt with their own racism. "We pretended it didn't exist. We didn't talk about blacks in a 'clean' way. I thought we should have done consciousness-raising among black women and white women, to discuss our feelings about race. I can't believe we'll ever come together until we talk about feelings." I asked her what she meant by "feelings."

"*Not* abstractions," she replied. "I'd like to share personal experience. For example, when I was a kid, a black woman came to iron. I thought she was beautiful and angelic. At the same time, I was always aware of the fact that she was a servant. It's hard for me to talk about things like this with black women, but I think we all have to try. At school, kids used to call me 'nigger lips.' I'd like to talk about the feelings we have about our bodies, too. Sometimes, with individual black women, I feel some kind of honesty happening, and mutual affection, too. But I don't feel the honesty *or* the affection in groups."

Still another white woman claims not to have "a grain of prejudice against black people—the ones that are like me, that is." Quick to hear the condescension in her words, she defended herself by adding: "I know how that sounds, but, after all, that's the way I choose white friends, too; I choose qualities I find endearing." I asked her what she thought had inhibited frank communication at sex-roles meetings, and she responded, "We didn't solicit the opinions of the black women because we didn't want to focus on them as special cases, which would have been condescending. And the blacks were so protective of one another that honesty wasn't possible." "What were your own feelings about the black women?" I asked. "I felt they resented me," she said. "I know they feel inferior. I try to remember the pain they feel. I try to think, They don't really hate me, they hate themselves." And then she confessed that her own feelings were a complicated mixture of inferiority and guilt—"I'm politically unsophisticated, and naive, and ignorant, really, about the black struggle, so I was always afraid to speak out. I don't understand the rhetoric"—compounded with "a vague feeling of superiority: at graduate school, when a black gets up in class to make a speech, I feel sure he's going to blow it and be incompetent." She paused to reflect whether that wasn't the same assumption men were likely to make about women, and added, "It really makes me feel good when I hear a black woman who's being smart and logical. I know that's patronizing"; she added impatiently, "if a man said that about a woman I'd be angry. But what can I do? I'm in a class with a lot of blacks, and I feel that I should pretend to be less smart and less good at things than I am. I don't want to show them up. You tell me," she said, "if that's guilt or inferiority or superiority." She laughed. "What it is, is a mess. And the other thing is," she went on, "at the same time, they frighten me."

"I was angry all the time when black women were present," another woman—whose anger had not yet cooled down—said. "I felt unjustly judged all the time. Their pain has made them neurotic; they're quick to see slights that aren't there. OK, so we're privileged. That doesn't mean that we're racist, too. After all, why would we choose to send our kids to Woodward if we were racist? Can you imagine anyone thinking we'd invite a black kid over just to *prove* something? What nonsense." I asked her why she hadn't allowed her anger to surface: "I was gutless," she said. "I waited for somebody to say something, instead of being overwhelmed by guilt or by rhetoric." Her answer as to whether or not guilt was an appropriate response was a decided "No. It's too easy. They scream at us—and we sit there feeling guilty instead of working together. We encourage polarization by being afraid to say what we think." "What should the white women have done?" I asked. "We should have said, 'Look, we like you. Cut the bullshit. Stop accusing us of being racist. Lay the blame where it really belongs.' "

White women very much resist and resent being called *privileged* (particularly by black women who are more or less in the same financial boat as they are); and black women tend to dismiss their resentment as poor-little-rich-girl nonsense. There is no denying that we are, by virtue of being white and middle-class, privileged in this society. While it serves no real purpose to deny that we're privileged, the white women's anguish at being "misunderstood" probably stemmed from their realization that privilege is often a terrible straitjacket, spiritually and emotionally confining, debilitating, and deforming. Nobody likes to hear privileged people complain (nothing is more gross, for example, than to be told by somebody really rich how adorable they'd have been if only they'd had the luck to have been born poor); but the truth is—everybody knows exactly what is meant by "the bird in the gilded cage"—a privileged woman is not the same as a free woman, that is, a woman with clearly perceived options. If the privilege which accrues to one as an accident of birth is not perceived and experienced as freedom, then—no matter how much like a bed of roses it may appear to someone else—it is simply not freedom at all. The stereotypical spoiled and pampered, doll-like, childlike Southern belle is privileged; but seen in terms of human freedom and potential, she is a grotesque (not necessarily a likable or sympathetic grotesque— victims are not "nice" simply by virtue of their victimization—but a grotesque nonetheless). Just as men are brutalized and de- humanized by their oppression of women, "privileged" white women have had to sacrifice some of their humanity in exchange for their "privilege." (A good question, of course, is whether, when it comes to the crunch, white women will be willing to sacrifice some of their privilege in exchange for more humanity.) Women are, quite naturally, not very eager to hear about the terrible things oppression has done to the oppressor—it's asking sainthood of any victim to ask that she extend compassion to the victimizer; and black women are, quite naturally, not keen to hear the wails of privileged white women.

I also think the plea "Stop accusing us of being racist. Lay the blame where it really belongs" is at the heart of the matter be- tween white and black women. The question of where "the blame" really belongs is what politics is all about; it's also what religion is all about—and both white women and black women speak of *blame* with such fervor and fire they might be talking about original sin. Politics and emotions were inextricably inter- woven in all our black-white confrontations . . . and for women who were just beginning to struggle to put "feelings" into a polit- ical context, it was difficult to know where to put "the blame"— particularly as we had not, really, even defined the exact nature of the crime.

Here are two very different views of the black-white experience at Woodward. Both women speaking are white:

"The black women made criticisms as if they were observers,

not participants. They made themselves impossible to include. Naturally white women were defensive. Black women threw their weight around. They knew we wanted and needed them, so they enjoyed their power. They enjoyed the advantage our guilt gave them." This woman feels it is impossible for her to have any relationships with black women, the reason being that "they act as if they don't know me—they put me down." She also believes that "the sex-roles group handled black-white relationships just fine. We reached out, we asked, we informed—sometimes, in fact, we went overboard and were obsequious. After you make a courteous invitation, that should be the end. Don't treat them like prima-donnas. Our relationships are just about as good as white-black relationships can be at this time, which isn't saying much. But I'm not willing to turn myself inside out for the privilege of being called a racist."

Far from feeling that the group "handled black-white relations just fine," another woman says, "There was very little sympathy on the part of the group as to where black parents were. Did we ever say to them, 'What do you want?' We didn't. We told them where it was. I think a lot of people didn't really care what black parents thought. I know it's hard to reach out, but why couldn't we have said, 'Look, it's *important* for us that you come. We want you.' We *did* want them. But we never spoke to them frankly. We didn't ask direct questions." When I asked her whether she thought the anger of white women accused of racism was justified, she said: "We were angry because the blacks didn't see sex roles as a priority. It's absolutely true that when they did come to meetings, the conversation just swirled around them. Naturally the blacks thought that the feminist issue took people away from their cause. When I said that I thought black-white relationships were more important than male-female relationships, I was put down for not being feminist enough. But I believe that you can't just focus on your own oppression. Maybe I can't fight the black struggle, but I can support it. I can keep it in my head as a priority. The group didn't do that."

This is the perspective of one black woman: "I don't think the sex-roles people were racist. But I was angry because I thought they would never see racism as the all-important, all-pervading issue. They see the women's Movement as being of overwhelming

importance; and we see racism as being of overwhelming importance, and that's that. I thought they gave us prima-donna treatment. That's damned condescending. They were oversolicitous;
they had that 'Take the veil from our eyes' attitude. But that was
because they didn't really regard us as equals, or as partners, you
understand. Whites listened to blacks as if everything they said
was gospel. And you *know* they didn't *really* believe it, which
made me have contempt for them. It doesn't take a lot of sense to
realize that blacks often say things just to needle and provoke
and incite. But you people got sucked in every time. Why did
you fall all over yourselves when guilt was laid on you? You felt
you were paying your dues just by feeling guilt, and that was
that. I don't want to be pandered to because I'm black. We have
real problems to work at. When black women are doing their
thing by showing off and whites do their thing by accepting
guilt, we're nowhere. Blacks said, 'I can't make you see it because
you're white.' That's too damned easy. Somebody must have told
you anger was racist—which is stupid; because you just drank it
in when somebody said something like that. And another thing, I
felt pushed and pressured to come to meetings. I wanted to be
left alone. One engraved invitation is enough."

Even in retrospect, we can agree only on one point: we were
not honest. Nobody was.


The sex-roles women who were working on the media presentation—which included video-taped commercials, television programs, and skits demonstrating the different ways in which boys
and girls were introduced to their roles and made, subtly, to
conform to them—invited several black women to see the fruits
of their labor. They were concerned to see whether the black
women wished to add to or subtract from the presentation, and
also whether the black women would endorse the presentation.
That meeting, in contrast to the other, was not an acrimonious
one. In fact, project-oriented meetings were much more successful than meetings which were not anchored to concrete work
happenings. The black women did endorse the presentation.
There was no substantive disagreement, just as there had been
no substantive disagreement as to the facts and evidence pre-

sented by the Feminist Book Collective. What the black women
wanted for their female children—independence, resourceful-
ness, assertiveness, and a recognition of options available to them
—differed not at all from what the white women wanted for
their female children. There is reason to believe that the black
women's objections, all along, were based less on the philosophi-
cal underpinnings of feminism or on articulated feminist goals,
than on various public statements issued by the Women's Liberation Movement, which failed to take into account the complexities of their own dual struggle as blacks and as women. They also
objected to what they perceived as the middle-class bias of
Movement women, to differences of style and emphasis, and also
to the fact that—as they saw it—white women valued their own
pain above that of their black sisters. They saw us suddenly on
fire with zeal for our own cause, and realized with justifiable
bitterness that we had never been so ardent on their behalf.


I have spoken at length to several black women since then, and I
think that what they have to say (and they never really said this
as a group to the sex-roles group) partially explains why we had
the difficulties we had. If, somehow, these things had been said
and thrashed out at the outset, I think we would not have seen
each other as weapons for inflicting pain. The interviews that
produced these comments were often combative. The questions I
asked—Do you think women are oppressed? Who is "the
Enemy"? Do you agree that a black woman should "walk two
steps in back of her man"? Are Woodward women racist? Do
black women absorb the anger of black men that should be
directed at the system? Do you think black women and white
women can work together if they recognize their common oppression?—often reflected my own confusion. To a lesser degree,
the answers of the three black women, Barbara Mask, Terry
Babb, and Marge Hammock, reflected theirs. We were all exploring our own racial and sexual consciousness, and that struggle
inevitably produced a certain amount of inconsistency. But—
confusions and inconsistency notwithstanding—these women
speak so eloquently and so vigorously of their own necessities
and their own pain that I present their words as I heard them,

with no interpolations. I took issue with them when we talked (and will no doubt fight with them again); but I would be ashamed to quibble with their testimony:

Barbara Mask is an anatomist, and mother of two Woodward children and a preschool girl. I admired her, when I first met her at Woodward, because she seemed to me to be absolutely "together," cool and detached and almost intimidatingly capable. Her elegance, her poise and her formidable social grace led me to believe that nothing could possibly daunt her (an example of the error of judging by "style"). I now like her for very different reasons—not the least of which is her wry humor. Once she allows you to get past the polished defensive surface, Barbara is warm, relaxed, and expansive; it's hard to imagine her ever doing a mean thing. This is what she had to say:

"What can I possibly care what Germaine Greer has to say about women wearing knickers or not wearing knickers? Trivia! I didn't go to more sex-roles meetings because when I listened to those girls talk, I thought, I'm way ahead of them and their preoccupation with their problems. I've always assumed people had, within them, the power to change. I didn't think they were oppressed; I thought they were cowards. One woman said that when she graduated from college, she felt she had to get married. She couldn't see any options. I said to myself, She's free, white, and twenty-one, what does she mean, she has no options? She didn't *have* to get married. All those women could have changed their lives. Psychological cowardice stopped them, not oppression. Real oppression is where the whole system is against you. I know what you're going to say, that the male system is against them as women. But I can't feel that a woman like that is oppressed in the way that blacks are. I think they have shallow perceptions of oppression. They whine. OK, after I got over my irateness I recognized that they were talking about being brought up in a psychological halter that prevented them from seeing their options. It *still* annoys me to be confronted with shallowness. Women are probably the most oppressed people in the world, but there's a difference between being oppressed and loved—which you are when you're white—and oppressed and black. When you're black you're hated, scorned, looked at as a despicable thing. Maybe it's just as stifling to be a white woman, but how do I know? At least white women don't feel despicable; they don't feel like horrible ugly things, do they? You know, white people don't like *black* black people. I was always an acceptable black . . . reasonably clean and good-looking. I made it. And even that was insulting and disgusting. You know—not being 'like the rest of them.' My feeling about oppression is so emotional . . . every time a white woman talked about oppression, I was contemptuous. I thought, *How dare they?* Now when I get analytical, I know women are oppressed, and that black women are the most oppressed women in the world. But that word *oppression* in white mouths drives me crazy. Maybe if we could find another word it would be different. But I've never associated being oppressed with anything other than being black. I feel as if I could deal with the business of being a woman if I didn't have to deal with racism too. I relate everything to black and white. White people set the standards for beauty. If white women hate their looks and their bodies and internalize hate, how do you think we feel? I consider white women my oppressors as much as white men—if you're talking about classes, that is—actually I relate to individuals as individuals. I can say abstractly I hate whites, while, in fact, I like a lot of whites. Let's just say they're the ruling class and I hate them for that . . . and I don't think white women are any less racist than white men. They're in collusion, in fact. Think how many black men, women, and children white women have power over. Do you think it's any better to work in a white kitchen than to work under a white foreman? I've worked for men whose wives thought I had to be interested in their ugly fat old men (they weren't even good scientists! I was their assistant, and I was a better scientist than any of them), just because I was black. I guess they thought I had to be promiscuous because I was black. Yes, I see how even that can be interpreted as a 'woman's problem' . . . that those women saw their husbands as their identity and their security. But do you really think if white women would stop competing for men and recognize their own exploitation they'd be brought closer to black women? I doubt it. I don't know if the women's Movement can bring us together. I doubt it.

"Sure I agree about day care, and abortion, and equal pay. But

would white people want their kids in a day-care center with
black and Puerto Rican kids? For most white women nothing is
as dreadful as associating with blacks. Now that you mention
abortion . . . I was brought up Catholic and didn't see abortion as
an option. It was there, of course, but the people I knew couldn't
avail themselves of it because of internal brakes. Are you telling
me that there's an analogy between that and the woman who
couldn't see that she didn't have to get married? Well, maybe.
No one can tell me women are terrific. Women spat and threw
rocks at Little Rock and in New Orleans. No, don't tell me their
problem was they saw their identity in their kids and they felt
their kids were threatened. Their problem was racism. How
come it's only blacks that threaten them?

"As for all that talk about careers in the Movement—what kid
wants to be a latchkey kid? Who cares about black kids? People
who work want not to; people who are with kids want not to be.
We all—black *and* white women—romanticize the other side.
We have to do what we need to do for our own survival. And
then we justify it. Kids are a pain in the ass part of the time, and
jobs are a pain in the ass part of the time. . . . Options. Now,
when you say options, I can dig it. Because men don't have the
option to nurture they have to despise and caricature it . . . why
is 'housewife' a pejorative word? When I wasn't working, I
didn't have any fun at parties . . . people thought I was dull.
When I could say I was doing brain research, that made people
listen. But I was still *me*. I wasn't any more interesting, I'd just
gained status. That made me mad.

"Don't talk to me about that black long-suffering woman who
takes abuse from her husband to absorb his anger toward the
world—she's a fiction. It's a *white* fiction: you people either kill
us or mythicize us. Families ought to soothe one another, that's
OK. Sure, the effects of racism on the black man were diluted by
his woman . . . any kind of negative effect on anybody is diluted
by warmth. That's not a bad thing. I don't think a black woman
partner offering comfort in a relationship is helping to perpetuate
racism. No, I don't want to hear that if black women allowed
black men to put their anger where it belongs—against employers or the system—it would make a difference. It wouldn't make
any kind of difference.

"How do I feel about the people who say 'Black women should walk two steps behind black men'? Fooey. I feel about that the way I'd feel about any old wives' tale—contemptuous! That nonsense that black women are stronger than men is another old wives' tale. The black family is not matriarchal. The black father is a typical family despot. He over-mimics whites, that's his trouble.

"I don't want to hear any more nonsense about how black men suffer more than black women. Is there something about a man's psyche that makes him hurt more when he's wounded? When somebody says to me, Be a pillar of strength, I say, Uh huh, you want me to be a doormat. Sure, black men are sexist. Even the black men I know who respect women still mouth sexist clichés. Women are degraded. I don't like that any more than you do.

"Sure, I want the school to be aware of sexist attitudes. As to whether white women and black women can work together . . . we can have shared goals, but I don't know whether we can have friendship. If we can raise children who are not crippled, maybe we all have a chance."


Marge Hammock (a community and social worker) is an imposing, assertive, handsome woman who I believe could stare down any enemy and make him shrivel just by an act of will. No doubt Marge, who is justifiably contemptuous of the proclivity of some whites to romanticize blacks, will have something to say about this comparison, but it nevertheless suggests itself to me with some urgency: I remember seeing a movie with Anna Magnani, once, in which that lady held up a hand to a rearing horse and commanded him to stop rearing; for anyone else to have done that would have been laughable, but Magnani got away with it. Marge Hammock is one of the few women in the world, I think, who could be equally convincing in that hard-to-play situation. In fact, Marge told me she once sent a would-be rapist on his way with a frontal attack and a lecture. I believe it. Even when Marge unbends—and she is generous in her friendship—one is conscious of being with a woman with strong powers in reserve:

"I connect everything up with how it affects me as a black

woman. For example, if I hear white Movement women wanting stronger laws against rape, I think to myself, *they've used that one before—they just want an excuse to hang black men.* A white man coercing a dependent black woman is rape too. I'd like to hear somebody get excited over that! I can think of worse things than being abused sexually. I've suffered worse humiliations. The sex act isn't the worst thing or the best thing that can happen. You white people think too much of the sex act. As far as I'm concerned, rape is sleeping with a white man.

"Yes, I'm opposed as a woman; what's new about that? As far as the Movement is concerned, I don't have a position. I'm not negative, but I'm not committed; and I don't want to be forced into a position. I have suspicions about some of those 'ladies.' Men did not create a racist society all by themselves. The women got their goodies from a racist and sexist society, too. Only at the point at which it became unbearable did they start to protest.

"We can work together on substantive issues, and forget the ideology. We should be working together to force the staff to open up to change.

"Yes, black women need to find an identity for themselves, but, as Imamu Baraka says, 'Nationtime begins with family time.' We don't have enough time with our families. Our problem is to give ourselves to our spouse or our man and our children without getting caught up in the whole Miss Ann 'lady' nonsense. Getting out of the home has very little meaning—for us, the opposite has to be true; you know, keeping kids alive in the public-school system is a twenty-three-hour-a-day job. My mother took care of rich white kids. When she was asked what she wanted for Christmas, she said, 'to be alone with my family.' Service to her family was the only thing whites could not benefit from, you see. If the women's Movement interprets freedom as leaving kids, while black women are fighting to keep their kids, there is no way. . . . *Options* is a word I can understand. I don't want to get hung up on an either/or situation.

"I know you all have this idea that if a black man is mad at his boss, he kicks his wife. What you don't know is that the woman kicks back. It may be true that she dissipated his anger; it's also true that if the black man said to her, Shit, I'm tired, she said, Shit, I'm tired too, right back. If the black man said to her, I'm

going to kick that nigger in the ass today, she said, Not today, I
got kids to feed. You have this idea that the black woman acted
as the sponge for her man's anger. But the same woman who
dressed her man down for raisin' sand with his boss wound up
putting ground glass in the Man's pumpkin pie. Black women
have always been engaged in an underground war . . . to survive
. . . to keep the family alive. In slave revolts black women were
privy to all secrets; they were dumb, blind, and invisible, in the
master's bedroom. Black men were hung or shot . . . black
women were burned.

"Many of us feel that the anguish and the changes of white
women are not ours. . . . We got our back seat because we're
black, not because we're women. I don't consider myself the
prime victim. I consider the black man the prime victim. What
do I think about being told I have to walk two steps behind
black men? It's a game, it comes from the white community; like
they're hearing the Man say, 'To be powerful like me, you have
to control your women.' "

Terry Babb, who has a son at Woodward, is at graduate school at
Columbia. Several times she and I outraged each other at sex-
roles meetings. Terry was perhaps the most vehemently—sometimes violently—outspoken of all the black women on behalf of
Third World women. Every time she spoke, I thought, *We're
going to get it again.* And yet, when I spoke with her outside the
group—an encounter I was extremely apprehensive about—I felt
no animosity; on the contrary, I felt an earnest and eager desire,
on her part, to communicate, to be understood, and to understand me. I wondered often, within the group, if she actually
hated us; I knew, outside the group, that in fact we were closely
locked in struggle, and in pain. Her apparent contentiousness
came, I believe, from despair, and not from rancor at all. She is
extremely sensitive to real or imagined slights; she smarts and is
galled by lack of awareness and concern.

"I'm able to see that sexism is a problem in society. It's true I'm
usually so concerned about racism, I haven't got time. . . . But
when I can see the possibility of our daughters' being damaged
. . . like a sixth-grade girl 'not interested' in math, I can dig it. But

I got turned off the sex-roles meetings. Too much stuff about blocks and dolls. I get tired of talk. I'd like to work on projects. I thought the group's video-tape presentation was great. I'd like to work on taping oral history of women . . . like my grandmother, who's been a houseworker all her life. She told me she'd always had 'kind' employers. The truth is they broke her health and took her away from her own kids, and she didn't even know she'd been had.

"I never had any quarrel with you people on substantive issues. I did feel men were being attacked. It wasn't what you said, it was the tone. You know I never will attack a black man or confront him in public. There just aren't enough black men around . . . they go to the war, and they come home in caskets, or they're lost to drugs. White men heap garbage on us all—black men, black women, and white women alike.

"I know people got mad at me when I said white women threaten black men's jobs. Well, it's true, if black men get their asses in the street, *I'm* in trouble. I'm not saying that white women shouldn't have jobs, I'm saying that you should see the issue with all its implications. I know I didn't say that at the meeting; I was too angry. I get angry when white middle-class women don't see Third World problems. I think we need a complete thrust at American society—at racism, sexism, and class.

"You know, I get angry when I see a white male attack a white woman. If I didn't make it clear at meetings that I thought sexism was a problem, it was because I was impatient with you. You kept trying to convert us to the issues, when that was never really at stake—you had us there with you all along. It was your *attitude* that hurt; you just weren't sensitive to our needs. . . . Of course I've experienced sexism in my own life. I go to Columbia, a sexist institution if there ever was one; I'm practically having a heart attack: men dominate the social sciences; women are the worker ants. Of course I'm oppressed psychologically and sexually. Men murder me with logic. . . . Sure it's true that black men go to work and get the shit and the fallout is on black women. How do I feel about walking two steps behind a black man? Side by side, baby, or nobody walks at all.

"If I had to say who the enemy was, I'd say white society, dominated by white men. Still, it makes me mad that all the gains blacks have made are eclipsed by media attention to the Lib. . . . Are white women as culpable as white men? I get mixed up. . . . I say a woman should be sensitive. She should know how a black woman feels. She hates to clean? How does she think we feel? She doesn't want her kids brutalized? Look what they've done to ours. Now you want to get off your pedestal. Terrific. You dug it for a long time, though. We never had the luxury of being dependent children. Of course I've been oppressed by black men . . . men who were mean and evil and brutalized women and children. I absolutely agree that women are oppressed. No doubt about that. But I think in terms of ethnicity first. I think of hunger, of sick kids. . . . We'd better fight for one another's oppression. When you said, 'I'm going to fight for my own revolution this time,' I thought, Where the hell is she at? We're getting put behind again."

Terry Babb, Marge Hammock, and Barbara Mask agreed that women are oppressed (although the word *oppression* is, when not used in conjunction with black suffering, often offensive to them); and they all agreed that Woodward needed to examine its attitudes and its curriculum with regard to sexism: "If we can raise children who are not crippled, maybe we have a chance," they felt, and "We should work together to force the school to open up to change." They are all project-oriented: "We can have shared goals. I don't know if we can have friendship." "We can work together on substantive issues and forget the ideology." "I'd like to work on projects. . . . I never had any quarrel with you people on substantive issues."

These attitudes form the basis of a wary issue- and project-centered alliance of black and white women. As individuals, some of us have entered into generous (though unpredictable) friendships; as groups, we have been able to come together to exert pressure on Woodward, because it is pragmatic and expedient for us to do so. The presentation the Sex-roles Committee made to the staff in June, 1971, had the backing and support of the black women. Papers were, in fact, modified and expanded to reflect black women's experience as well as the experience of white women. More white women now see the importance—not just the tactical correctness, but the *rightness*—of attending and supporting Black Studies programs and presentations. We may not all see our interests as indivisible and our needs as organically related all the time, but we are often able to join forces. Jointly, we are forming a skills-resource bank. We plan jointly to tape oral histories of white women and black women, immigrants, daughters and granddaughters of slaves, and women who have made the difficult transition from the rural South to the urban North. As we explore our history and our heritage and reclaim the past together, perhaps we can better understand what has brought us to this present place where we so often fail to perceive one another's pain, and where we are trapped in historical animosity and fear.

I am forced to conclude that the experience of black women and white women at Woodward taught us all something that it will certainly be painful to come to terms with: it taught us that, as feminists, we are obliged to arrive at a synthesis of politics and emotion that is terrifyingly hard work. Because I am not, by temperament, a True Believer—to me, cynicism and the ability to doubt are attractive, even ennobling qualities, and I abhor fixated Perfect Explanations—I have tended to resist political definitions and solutions. But the questions raised at Woodward —Who is the enemy? Who are one's natural allies? What is the relationship between the class struggle, racism, and sexism?—are not going to be answered by "feelings," however much these may be informed by generosity and goodwill. If we are really going to have a revolution (and we must decide if that is what we want), we will each and all have to form a rigorous feminist analysis of our own. We must, that is, create a politics of our own. To insist that "feelings," and the integrity of the individual, will carry us through is useless, because in all our human converse words like *enemy* and *blame* keep cropping up. How can we talk to one another until we've identified the enemy, and placed the blame? To identify the enemy, and to place the blame, is necessarily to formulate a political philosophy . . . it can't be played by ear. But the political analysis or philosophy we formulate cannot be a system of belief or a blueprint for action that denies or contradicts our own experience, or our own emotions. So we must undertake to create a viable political analysis, which is at the same time a morality, of our own. It is not only for the sake of a far-off "revolution" that we must do so; it is also so that we can talk to one another and each know what the other means, so that we will not be imputing blame to one another wrongfully, and so that friendships may flourish and enrich us all. Our experience at Woodward taught us that all friendships are political, that love itself is a political act. Certainly we must always remember that each individual is a mystery and a riddle never to be solved or penetrated completely by another human being (else we presume, we judge motives, we play God); but we also need—in order to *see* one another—clarity. And clarity, the clarity without which love, friendship, revolution, and grace are impossible, demands a political definition of our past, our present, and our imagined moral future.

# 7

# Men and Women

"I'm a revolutionary by disposition and ideology, and yet in the two most important insurgencies of our time—that of women and that of blacks—I have no place."

"I came to sex-roles meetings, but I felt that the women were not reacting to me. My ego was hurt. I felt excluded. I couldn't understand the code. I felt like an outsider."

"I thought the Sex-roles Committee would help my daughter. I was indifferent to what 'good' it might do to my boys—after all, they had it good anyway. I was like the WASP who recognized that there was a 'Jewish problem' but who thought things would be fine if only the Jew—not the WASP—changed . . . or like Professor Higgins: 'Why can't a woman be more like a man?' "

The men speaking are feminists, married to feminists. They were not active in the Sex-roles Committee, yet the women's Movement has effected profound changes in their thinking and in their lives, and they wrestle with the implications of it daily.

Bart Meyers told me that he had not needed to be convinced that Woodward had to change in its attitudes toward boys and girls. "I had a daughter in kindergarten, and when I spoke to her teachers about changing the topography of the classroom to make the woodworking table accessible to girls—Joanie worked at it only when I was there to act as her protector—I was told that noisy play had to be separated from quiet play. The block area, which she had to pass on her way to the woodworking table, was a place where boys played wild and rough; it was called the 'boys' room,' in fact. Now why does playing with blocks have to be noisy? Why does playing with dolls have to be quiet? The idea is supposed to be that kids can enact 'human dramas' with dolls; well, people *are* noisy, so why can't doll-play be noisy?" He did not think the block-and-doll question was "trivial": "Dolls are given to girls to prepare them for their role in the nuclear family. In some schools, boys are punished by being sent to the doll corner, so they grow up thinking that they're trapped into love relationships, and into marriage, too. They feel they're punished again, among the 'dolls.'

"At home," Bart said, "we direct play—and we did so before the Sex-roles Committee. We're very careful in the toys we buy for the children. I don't allow guns, for example; I'm not a pacifist, but I think guns and killing aren't fun and games, they're a sad, serious business, and our son as well as our daughter should know that. We discourage our daughter from wearing dresses, because they have to be ironed, and we think she should understand that her mother doesn't want to spend her valuable time ironing." (Bart good-naturedly laughed when I pointed out to him that he had slipped automatically into speaking of ironing as "mother's work.")

"Also," he continued, "the kind of clothes Joan wears condition the kind of play that's possible. Twelve-year-old girls can't run. I used to wonder why girls ran 'funny,' until my wife (Mimi Meyers) showed me: they have to keep their thighs together and their legs apart so their underpants won't show."

I asked Bart if he had observed "innate differences" in his children. "My observations were that at the age of two and three our boy and girl were equally aggressive, but in spite of us they're being socialized differently. My son watches football, for instance, where all the players in an aggressive sport are men. What conclusions can he draw from that?" Bart, who teaches psychology at Brooklyn College, has personally experienced "women's work," a lot of which he's taken on since Mimi has gone back to graduate school. Did he like it?

"My own experience tells me that you can observe women working at their 'roles' and read all you like about what it's like to have a schedule imposed on you by your children, but unless you're doing it yourself, it's easy to think 'women's work is a cinch.' This year, while my wife has been back at school, I've done the shopping, and the cooking, I've taken care of the kids, and done the chores. A lot of it is a pain in the ass, and it's *no cinch*. I always helped, but now, I think I *share*. We have a real division of labor."

Hirsch Grunstein, who is married to Andrea Ostrum, said that when Gertrude Goldstein casually mentioned that girls don't seem to take to math and physics the way boys do at twelve or thirteen, it was "like a punch in my nose. To think that my daughter might be coming home with little-girl cuteness at the age of twelve, when at the age of five she was avid with curiosity about the world," shook him. "I had seen the 'girls' at the office typing meaningless memos, or serving coffee—they were the 'service' people. The logical conclusion of my daughter's dropping out from academic pursuits was that *she* would probably spend her life serving coffee and typing out memos dictated by pompous men."

I asked Hirsch how the women's Movement had affected his thinking. "I had always thought femininity did not have to enhance itself with an incapacity to function," he said. "But I used to see it as an individual, not a generic problem. I'm guilty of that standard phrase—whenever I liked a woman, I'd say, 'You're not like other women.' I always understood that women were discriminated against, but the women's Movement is what made me politically aware of the internalization of their oppression. It made me understand how societal expectations can change not only a woman's life, but her emotions as well.

"Am I an oppressor? Generically and socially, yes. I do benefit from the fact that women are oppressed, whether or not I want to. It's nice to be served. I often slide back into the old roles,

from habit, laziness, all those old reflexes. . . . What I would like
for my sons is for them to be totally free of the desire to be
served by anyone. They should build a life around the principle
'I am not served by anyone.' It would make their marriages a
completely different contract. Inasmuch as they will know they
have to tend to all of their own needs, their expectations and
their attitude toward their wives will be completely different,
and the composition of the family will change totally—there will
be fewer children, perhaps."

I asked Hirsch—who ponders his words carefully and speaks
with precision and formal European grace—whether he would
be pleased if his daughter chose to be primarily a wife and
mother.

"Well, nurturing is good work; but it doesn't *have to be*
women's work. It's more valuable than writing an esoteric poem,
but it doesn't have to be 'prettified.' If my daughter made the
choice to be a mother, if she were one of those rare women for
whom it is a real vocation, I would not be displeased—although
perhaps I should qualify that—if she were paid for her work, I'd
feel better. A woman dependent displeases me. In this world,
money makes you independent. If mothering had an official recognized status and income, I'd like it better. Would I want my
son to be just a father? When I reverse it like that, I see that it's
not right, because he'd be dependent; someone else would be
providing the bread. So looking at the reflected image, I must say
it's not OK for my daughter—here I am, wasping out the Jew
again—I can see my daughter's situation more clearly when it's
reflected in my son's."

Was he at all uneasy, I asked Hirsch, about the consequences
of interfering with societal norms?

"I have fears. Sometimes we tend to overlook the human needs
of our girls because of our conviction and zeal and the need to
redress wrong. My daughter was always loaded with Prince
Charming-and-Cinderella stories, with dolls, a pink room, and
ribbons, till she was six. We can't suddenly take it all away from
her. To make her feel that Barbie is bad—when Barbie is something she has been programmed to want and wants very much—
would only hurt her and make her feel there is something wrong
with her for wanting it. You can't just erase a prior identity. I feel

the same way about boys and guns. If you insist that they can't play with them, the guns become objects of fierce desire. I feel the child's needs have to be taken into consideration. If you derogate a sexist television program that they're watching and enjoying, they feel that you're putting *them* down. And of course I think of homosexuality, but that may reflect general male fears about masculinity. My fears existed before feminism, and homosexuality did too. Rationally, why should we suddenly think that feminism might foster homosexuality? It's probably the rigidity and polarization of sex roles that mess us up and make us uptight. People panic when they are faced with emotions they think are 'inappropriate.' I'd think, if anything, feminism would free people from having to go to polar extremes.

"It will take several generations before we know what feminism has wrought. I think of myself as the generation of the desert—all I think I can do is position my children to do the rest of the work—I have been incapacitated to live with the total solution. I don't even know what that solution would be."

Men were not invited to early Sex-roles Committee meetings. This was a decision committeewomen were often called upon to justify, and one which, in fact, I initially found off-putting. Later, however, I came to believe that the women were quite right not to have asked men to come to our first meetings: We are all so accustomed to looking to men for approval and validation, and we are used to deferring to men. Unsure of ourselves as we were in the early stages, we would have become self-conscious had they been among us.

"When meetings aren't structured," one man told me, "when they wander, I get lost. I need to know who is calling the meeting, and who is taking the initiative; I need an agenda. I went to two Sex-roles Committee meetings and I couldn't figure out what the unifying thread was. I felt disoriented."

As we settled down to project- and action-oriented meetings, many sex-roles committeewomen also felt the need for more structure, but our earlier meetings were indeed informal, free-wheeling, structureless and agendaless. Most men like things to appear "businesslike": they are more comfortable when meetings proceed according to rules and regulations. It's important for men to be able to define people hierarchically; they are sticklers for form and convention. They need to believe someone is in control.

Men behave, at meetings, as if they really believe that the shortest line between two points is a straight line . . . but they get very nervous if the "points" aren't absolutely declared and defined at the outset. (Which probably explains that staple of male conversation: those interminable raps about the best way to get from A to B by car. Men love road maps.) Women have been socialized to be less goal-oriented than men, who have to feel they know where they're going all the time. While that may get them what they want, or what they think they want, it also makes it hard for them to be spontaneous and hang loose.

Having delivered myself of all those irresponsible, Professor-Higgins-like generalizations (the temptation to think in simplifying stereotypes is nice to succumb to occasionally), I'll say what I know to be true: that sex-roles women, at early meetings, voyaged out on wild loops of undirected thought; their intense stream-of-consciousness talk was elliptical, and free. But we understood one another. We touched one another's nerves. I think we would have driven men crazy. There is no guarantee implicit in this kind of talk (except that everyone will become vulnerable to everyone else); and most men like results guaranteed. (This may well be a result of men's tendency to be analytic and women's tendency to think in "global" terms. Men seem to worry away at one particular aspect of a problem—often, it seems to me, boringly and ineffectually, but they can't let go, they have to feel that for every problem there is a solution—women, on the other hand, take into their consciousness all the elements in the field, including the emotional aspects . . . which leads to the male complaint, "She never gets to the point.")

One woman, defending the decision not to invite men to early meetings, said to me, "It's not so much that they're threatening. They're distracting. We'd have been taking care of them all the time, seeing that they had cream for their coffee, wondering if they were comfortable, making them feel they were important . . . *proving* things."

Men have traditionally assumed the role of protector of

women and children (a proclivity explained very tidily by Dorothy Sayers's Lord Peter Wimsey: "The desire to have all the fun
is nine-tenths of the law of chivalry"). Yet—and not really so
paradoxically—women often speak as if it were their wifely mis-
sion to protect their mates from the knowledge that they're not so
essential or powerful as they think they are, the he's-just-a-little-
boy-at-heart syndrome. I think what happens is that men take on
the burden, and exact the gratitude, for protecting women from
the world—from lightning, tidal waves, wars, and other men—
while women take on the burden of protecting men from themselves; that is, from a knowledge of their own insufficiencies. The
end result of this strange bargain is that women become the
sheltered vassals of males whose egos are nourished and intact.

Another woman said to me: "If men had come to early meetings, the first thing you know, they'd have elected a vice-presi-
dent and a treasurer, and we'd have spent hours discussing
whether to take out an insurance policy in case someone slipped
on a banana peel in a committeewoman's house." She added
grimly, "I know what I'm talking about. I belong to a neighborhood food-buying co-op, and when we started out, everything
was easy and unhassled—not slipshod or undisciplined, just un-
regimented and pleasant. We drove to the markets together, we
distributed the food among ourselves, and used the occasion for
socializing; we were saving money and having a good time. Then
a couple of husbands got involved. All of a sudden we were a
corporation. We were taking out special car-insurance policies,
we were using words like *default* and *liability*—and none of it
was necessary. It was inconceivable to us that any woman in the
group would rip off another; but the men had to have written
guarantees. It began to feel like war-games . . . boring nonsense,
but it made men feel important."

Another woman had a conflicting point of view: "I thought all
along the group was too unstructured," she told me, "I *wanted*
agendas. I'm busy; I don't like to waste time. I got the feeling,
when I pressed for more organization and discipline, that women
were accusing me of 'acting like a man.' Still, I do think these are
things women will have to work out for themselves and among
themselves. I think part of being a responsible adult is planning
and looking ahead. It used to drive me nuts when women went

off on tangents. It was OK in the early meetings, when we were feeling our way, but later on it got to be a mess, what with one woman talking about tactics while another woman was talking about feelings." This woman thought we should have had a rotating chairmanship, "and we'd have gotten a lot more done." Still, she felt that if we were ever going to learn how to direct our own lives, we couldn't have men acting like backseat drivers. "They'd have snowed us," she exclaimed.

We began to invite fathers to attend meetings in the spring of 1971, when we were preparing for our presentation to the staff. There were two meetings to which more than three or four men came. They were markedly different from those meetings attended by women only.

Looking back on the notes I took at one meeting, I find a note urgently scribbled by the woman sitting next to me: "All the men are talking," she wrote. She meant, *to the exclusion of all the women.* Ironically, the woman who wrote this is extremely articulate and persuasive, formidably intelligent and also full of grace. What she has to say is usually as remarkable for its charity as it is for its succinctness and aptness. She enjoyed the respect of the entire group. Nevertheless, at this particular meeting she spoke not at all. But her husband did. It was hard for anyone watching him not to believe that he was impatiently waiting for all those silly women to stop nattering so that he could tell them how to be liberated. It was extraordinary, in fact, how many verbal, assertive women did not attempt to express themselves at that meeting. Their expressions seemed to plead for tolerance for their husbands' pomposity, or chauvinism, or long-windedness. The women were—reflexively it seemed—protecting their mates. Most of the men present tended to pontificate or to preen. (I've since tried to find out from men if they feel diminished when their wives "act badly" at parties or meetings. Most men I spoke with appeared startled by the question, yet I know a woman would know immediately what I meant had I asked her the same question in reverse. The responses I got from most men seem to indicate that, while they have a certain pride of possession, they don't feel—as women would—that razor blades have been applied to the core of their being when their wives do something unbecoming in public. Mr. Mitchell will undoubtedly survive Martha's shenanigans, but a woman whose husband has publicly played the fool feels literally devastated, as if she has been robbed of her own worth.) The males at that meeting dominated the females, while the females ego-propped the males.

The men generally started off with abstractions. They talked of "the human condition," or "developmental levels"; and the women more often started with personal experience—"my son," or "my daughter," or "I."

There is a great deal of talk among feminists about the virtues of "talking from personal experience" as opposed to talking about "abstractions." In consciousness-raising groups, for example, one is urged to speak subjectively and specifically about one's personal experience and feelings, and to eschew generalizing, "theorizing," and talking in abstractions. This first-person rule may be a valid technique in consciousness-raising groups, particularly in the early stages, when women—many of whom have never been seriously listened to in a group before—are just finding their own voices, for a consciousness-raising group is a kind of sharing, not an argument. Many women profess to deplore abstract thought, and they are right in thinking abstractions are often a cop-out. If a man and a woman are talking, or fighting—about their marriage, for example—to throw abstractions into the conversation is often just a flight away from personal confrontation. On the other hand, if a husband and wife are discussing Marxism, or linguistics, or whether spaghetti originated in China or in Italy, they're not going to be able to do so *without* the use of abstractions (or facts; and it's amazing how often people, for the sake of argument, confuse *abstractions* with *facts* . . . so that when they say they deplore abstractions, they often really mean they don't want to be bothered with facts). Consequently, I think we fall into sloppy and dangerous thinking when we say that "abstractions" are male, and therefore to be despised. Similarly, we get tangled in mischievous nonsense when we express the converse belief: that anything "male" is superior to anything "female," and therefore to be emulated. I don't know why, if the meaning of liberation is that we find our own singular ways of being without regard to culturally imposed roles, we need to establish this either/or dichotomy. The unfettered, unfragmented brain should be truly androgynous. If women are in fact human beings, they ought to be able to differ, not only in opinion, as do male human beings, but in style. We ought each to be able to choose our own style. Certainly women are free to abhor abstractions, but they ought to do so, not on the grounds that abstractions are "male," but on the basis of personal preference and the appropriateness of abstractions to the matter at hand. Because we are just beginning to establish a world-view and analysis of our own, just beginning to see reality in other-than-male terms, feminists often get caught in two mutually contradictory propositions: one being that whatever characteristics are attributed to the dominant ("male") class are desirable and to be emulated; and the other, that whatever is female ("womanly") is more "human," loving, compassionate, and good. Thus we get bogged down in such futile arguments as whether it's "nicer" or "better" or "more important" or "more life-sustaining" to be in the kitchen; in the company of other women; baking bread, sharing companionable warmth, and exchanging mutual sympathy; or to be in the living room discussing philosophy or election returns with the men. The truth is, of course, that what's "nicer" or "better" or "more important" ought to be irrelevant to whether one is in the kitchen or the living room. One should be free to be where one wants to be on the basis of personal proclivity and interest, not on the basis of class or sex. Whether women as a class want to discuss philosophy ought not to influence the decision of one single human being, male or female, as to whether *he* or *she* wants to discuss philosophy. A sane world would have men and women in the kitchen, and women and men in the living room.

One of the aftermaths of the meetings with men at Woodward was that several sex-roles committeewomen chose to put men down for *talking in abstractions*; and I think that's unfortunate. There are good, pragmatic reasons for barring men from some kinds of feminist meetings: their presence does indeed make it harder, sometimes, for women to speak honestly and freely, and for women to break out of established roles and patterns. Moreover, for men to become the focus of a group by assuming adversary positions is not productive. Also, why shouldn't women group together in a cooperative, noncompetitive spirit? For one thing, it gives the lie to the male belief that we are incapable of generous friendship. Men certainly don't feel called upon to defend the privilege of bonding together—their own clubs are holy-secular institutions. I don't see that we really need to justify our decision to form homogenous groups with the dubious claim that "woman talk" is good and "man talk" is bad.

I wonder if one of the reasons many women feel uncomfortable with abstractions is that they have been zapped so often by men who tend to play it "cool" in arguments—that is, to divorce emotion from intellect—with a you're-too-emotional dismissal, implying that one can't be both logical and passionate at the same time?

To establish my own biases: I like talking about concepts, I like argument, and I like debate—I find it nourishing, and I find it exhilarating—I think it's fun. Also, I dislike the tendency to "psychologize" debate; that is, I'm usually much more concerned with apparent content than with inquiring into people's motives for espousing a particular point of view. (Not being God, I'm not likely to know what their motives are anyway.) I also admit, somewhat reluctantly, to enjoying flashy, clever, show-off talk. It doesn't sustain or enlighten, but it's nice to be amused. So, all in all, I rather enjoyed the meetings the men came to. I like a good fight and, since I wasn't married to any of the men in any case, I wasn't inhibited. It made me mad when they dominated the women, but on the other hand, I had fun listening to show-off arguments. And I thought some of the questions they raised were important and deserving of consideration and debate.

Two of the men who came to sex-roles meetings did not enjoy show-off arguments:

"There was gladiatorial skirmishing among men," Hirsch acknowledged. "We do it all the time—it's academic and verbal judo; the less verbal and articulate fall by the wayside. It's a contest. Ordinarily, I take part in it with relish. I love to demolish arguments, wrap up, or reconcile points of view. At those meetings, the men thought of the women as spectators, and the presence of an audience vitiates the substance of debate. I was disgusted with myself afterward. In the end, it's exhausting and depressing. Cleverness really is cheap. It's about as exhilarating as a high-school debate. Scoring points is frivolous. Wit and elegance must not be allowed to obscure what is right and what is wrong. I find verbal calisthenics repulsive."

I reminded Hirsch of one man who made a disingenuous disclaimer: "I don't express myself very well," he said, and then proceeded to express himself for twenty minutes.

"Well," Hirsch said, "that's the kind of disarming thing one says to women—it's calculated to play to their softness. We know women find it hard not to be 'nice.'"

Bart agrees that "The women at the meetings were certainly better informed than we were; they had a better feel for the issues. Nevertheless, at the two meetings I attended, the men tried to dominate. They were scoring points. The women were at various levels of consciousness, so some chafed when men missed the point, some were embarrassed. Most were charitable."

Most Woodward women agree that men tried to dominate the meetings they attended, but that control was wrested away from them by an act of communal will. There were some women, however, who did not see their presence as particularly trying:

"I didn't see the nature of the confrontation as men versus women, but as feminists versus nonfeminists," said one. "Nonfeminist women at the large meetings attended by men were just as distracting as men. I don't think the presence of men made any real difference, at least not to those women whose husbands weren't present. The men did their usual thing—made suggestions as if from an eminence—but I thought they were trying hard. They were reasonable, they were groping, and they were honest."

An example of the kind of "distraction" this woman was talking about was this clinker thrown into the conversation by a man during a discussion about aggression and intellectuality: "Why is it that we react more strongly to the fact that girls are verbally aggressive and boys hit, than we do to the fact that there are children starving in this world?" Hardly an example of elegant verbal calisthenics.

At one of the meetings we talked about the kinds of false equations people tend to make: sensitivity is equated with lack of assertiveness, just as strength is equated with violence. This kind of falsification allows antifeminists to say we are giving our daughters the opportunity to develop characteristics—such as violence—that we criticize in men.

"If I want my daughter to develop her physicality," one woman said, "to be strong . . . even if I want her to feel that she's able to fight back and win, that doesn't mean I'm sanctioning violence. What it does mean is that I don't want her to be raped because she's never been encouraged to defend herself. I want her to be physically self-sufficient, so that she can deal with the outside world."

One of the men—responding to questions at this same meeting about how young girls who already feel physically disadvantaged can be made to change their view of themselves—denigrated the hammer-and-screwdriver approach to helping girls achieve self-reliance: "Boys already have an edge with the hammer and the screwdriver. A thirteen-year-old boy has a thirteen-year head start, and a five-year-old boy has a five-year head start; they're hard to beat. If physicality is conceived as a battle, and girls lose, how will that help them? What big deal is it to master the screwdriver or the hammer anyway? Education is about excelling in math and physics, so why not encourage academic, rather than manual, excellence? Girls can excel academically if the expectations of the adults around them make that possible. Forget about the hammer and the screwdriver!"

A woman rejoined that academic achievement was not likely, in itself, to guarantee self-confidence and mastery, or to be a panacea; she had always had high grades in school, she said, and yet she felt like a patsy when she had to deal with the world of concrete matter. She had despised herself for not being athletic, and when she was with boys had always had to cover up the fact that she was intelligent.

Left to themselves, the women would, I think have continued to talk along these lines, drawing from their own experience, but at this point, a man responded to the antihammer proposition by saying that the male speaker's perception of the superiority of the pen to the hammer sprang from his class-consciousness, and that it was an elitist and privileged point of view. This was the kind of "abstraction" that made most women impatient and that they were not eager to pursue. They did not want to discuss class, nor contend with the charge that, by overrating intellectuality we were guilty of intellectual elitism. They insisted that the real issue was the freedom for boys and girls to choose freely from the screwdriver, the pen—or the frying pan.

Now, while it is indeed true to say that we would wish every human being to make an unhampered choice from among the frying pan, the hammer, and the pen, it is also somewhat simplistic. I wish that we had felt free to pursue the ramifications of the class argument, which is central, not peripheral, to the women's Movement—if the women's Movement is to be construed as political at all. On the other hand, I wish the men had felt free to speak from their own personal experience as well. The women of the Sex-roles Committee were concerned with the burdens sex-role stereotyping had placed upon their sons, as well as upon their daughters. Yet in neither of the meetings attended by men did the men discuss how *they* had felt as boys and young men, whether they had felt constricted or frightened by having to live up to the male superman image. The question that immediately occurred and remained unanswered was that if a woman felt "like a patsy" because she was unathletic, how must an unathletic man have felt? I think it would have been valuable to us all if we could have shared these experiences. Perhaps the men felt that the women would not have welcomed proof that men were oppressed by sex-role stereotyping too; women undoubtedly often doubt the sincerity of men who claim they are victims, considering that men have derived enough gratification and power from the status quo not to want to change it. Perhaps, on the other hand, the men were just unwilling to appear "weak" and to take the risk of vulnerability. In any case, we played our roles—the men spoke in abstractions, while the women spoke from personal experience. The self-disgust several men expressed at having engaged in verbal calisthenics, as well as the tendency of women to deprecate the ability to manipulate words and ideas probably sprang from a deficiency each sex perceives in itself: women are "good" at "feelings" and, as one man pointed out, are often over-whelmed, assuming the role of "spectators" in intellectual debate; men are good in debate, and "bad" at expressing feelings, a state of affairs which ought not to be seen as the occasion for sterile arguments about which is a better way to be, but as a potent argument for not channeling our children into stereotypical sex roles, an argument against aborting either the play of the mind or the exercise of the emotions.

I think, too, that the tendency to "psychologize" debate—a tendency which has little to do with gender stereotyping unless we choose to add it to the list of Freud's crimes—also confuses the issue, and makes people loath to enter into rational debate. If a Jesuit and an atheist are arguing, for instance, there are people far more concerned with trying to guess what their moth-ers and fathers might have done to their three- or four-year-old psyches that might have made them—respectively—a Jesuit and an atheist, than with weighing the relative merits of their argu-ments. Similarly, if a Marxist and a liberal are engaged in debate, instead of considering it a primary obligation to attend to *what* they're saying, many people consider it their primary obligation to second-guess *why* they're saying it. We have all had the expe-rience of being stopped dead in our argumentative tracks by someone responding to a passionate argument with "But have you thought about *why* you feel so strongly about that?" The implication being that anyone who holds strong opinions—about religion, art, politics, or whatever—is somehow suspect, and in need of amateur psychoanalyzing. This kind of dibble-dabbling in psyches, the conversion of argument into sensitivity courses, confuses and vitiates rational argument. It is a way of saying that nothing anybody says really matters because she, or he, really means or "feels" something else. It is another kind of fragmenta-tion, and it is as damaging in its way as the fragmentation of personality that evolves from sex-role stereotyping, and as dis-dainful of human expression as the imperatives imposed on us by a sexist society. Naturally we do all ask ourselves why we hold the beliefs we hold, but we have a right not to expect other people to supply the reasons.

In spite of difficulties of communication, however, the meet-

ings men attended helped to raise the consciousness of some
men. I like the reaction of one of the men present to the recount-
ing of an incident involving a Woodward girl who had been
refused service by a park-department food concessionaire because of her "abusive" language. (A Woodward boy had pushed
and shoved a girl at an ice-skating rink. The girl had retaliated
by calling him a four-letter word, and the concessionaire who
witnessed the incident later refused to serve the girl because
"ladies don't talk like that.") The man had listened to the girl's
mother tell her tale, and then commented: "When that mother
spoke I realized that I had always taken male aggression for
granted. If a boy hit a boy, I would say, *Well, boys will be boys.*
Of course I would have said it was stupid for a man not to serve
a girl because she used bad language, but my derogation of him
would have been in the benign mode. The mother of that girl
brought the boy's aggression into a completely different focus. I
suddenly saw how trapped the girl was. She had not been programmed to respond physically, to hit back; and it was also not
considered permissible for her to retaliate verbally. The indigna-
tion her mother manifested had the wrath and power of a
prophet. Her daughter had been denied any way out. It made
me realize that when I said to myself, *Boys will be boys*, I was
really saying, *Boys are stronger and dominant and better.* I
would never have done what that boy had done myself, because
I am not an aggressive man, but I had regarded it as nothing to
be indignant about either. I wasn't even really indignant at the
vendor because I accepted that this was the way things were.
However, if that same incident happened now I'd be angry. If it
happened to *my* daughter, I'd be angry. If there is a solution to
this problem, I don't think it is to make girls more aggressive or
to make boys less aggressive. The solution must be to have one
standard of behavior for all. I don't know if aggression is good or
bad. If it is good, let there be an equal amount for both sexes.
Personally, I would tend to decrease the level of aggression all
around. You can't skim some off the male side and add it to the
female side; it doesn't work like an algebraic equation."

I think this incident, and the way in which we, as middle-class
whites perceived it, is proof that to talk about class is not irrelevant to sex roles. As another of the men present pointed out,

the girl in question, had she been a working-class girl or brought up in a street-culture, might have acted very differently. She might very well have fought back physically, and she might have fought to win.

Finally, as we discussed our presentation to the school, some fathers argued that they should help determine the program and make the presentation to the staff, saying, "This is a human problem; we are all victims." The men-and-women-are-equally-victimized argument went hand in hand with the "practicality" argument: "Realistically, men have more clout; your approach to the staff will have more weight if men share the platform." It did not seem to us that men could logically argue both that they were as victimized as women, and that they had more weight or more power than women. If they were willing to surrender their power, the first step would be for them to acknowledge that women would have to speak for themselves. After all, it was women, not men, who had questioned the status quo in the first place. It was women and their daughters who had the most to gain, or to lose. We were accused of being more concerned with our own egos than with the welfare of our children, but our point of view prevailed.

Woodward men who espouse the feminist cause have been, since then, supportive; the women have determined policy, goals, and tactics.

No one, I think, denies that sex-role stereotyping in our society is a human problem that has grievously afflicted men as well as women, just as slave-holders were as damaged in their humanity as the slaves whose lives they controlled. But, while both oppressed and oppressor may be equally brutalized, the thrust for radical change comes from the oppressed. The reins must be kept in the hands of the oppressed, because implicit in the struggle is the need for the subordinate class to direct its own ascension.

Our yearning is for one another, but it is rare even for the best of lovers to be the best of friends. We can be lovers and sex partners, teachers and pupils, protected and protectors; but men and women have always found it terribly difficult to be comrades, playmates, and generous, honest friends. Men and women are not equals, and true friendship is a relationship of equals. It is not necessary for friends to be the same—differences provide the zest in friendship—but it is necessary that friends be, and be deemed, equal. It is hard for both sexes to unlearn ways of being that have been operative for centuries, validated by the culture, and internalized so well that they seem to spring from nature, to have been bred in the bone and marrow. Out of the struggle for change at Woodward have emerged some genuine friendships between men and women, in spite of the prohibitions of caste; I think that is a rare and wonderful achievement.

# 8

# June 1971:
# A New Beginning

> . . . If then at first wise Nature had
> Made women either good or bad,
>    Then some we might hate, and some choose;
> But since she did them so create
> That we may neither love, nor hate,
>    Only this rests: All, all may use.
> —JOHN DONNE

Group consciousness-raising had been limited by our decision to work assiduously at providing materials for the staff; but from time to time, teachers who had not met previously with the committee came to talk with us, and individual sex-roles committee-women continued to explore the implementation of nonsexist education in their classrooms with individual members of the staff. By the time the group met for its year-end presentation to the staff in June, 1971, there was probably not one member of the staff who had not reexamined his or her attitudes toward sex roles. The Sex-roles Committee and the staff had not met together as a group, however, since their earlier unpleasant confrontation; and we were apprehensive. We knew that the response we met with would be an index of what we might look forward to in the year to come. We had chosen, in spite of the strenuous urgings of several committee members, not to use an encounter-type session as a vehicle for our final presentation to the staff. Most of us felt that year-end-weary teachers might feel imposed upon, manipulated, or threatened by such a demand on their emotional energies. Nevertheless, we knew that this meeting would be more than a presentation of papers. It would be an encounter in all but name. We had no real way of taking the pulse of the staff, so we did not know what to expect from them, and somehow the sense of drama we all felt as we assembled for the final meeting of the year was heightened by the kind of weird half-life of a school empty of children and therefore bereft of its purpose, resembling some great hulking hibernating animal waiting for the return of vitality and life.

In order to enter the auditorium for the Sex-roles Committee workshop presentation, staff members had to open a door on which this Moslem edict was posted:

INFIDELS, DOGS, AND WOMEN MAY NOT ENTER.

Inside, the auditorium was oaktag-papered with wall-to-wall quotations:

"I find more bitter than death the woman, whose heart is snares and nets, and her hands as bands . . . One man among a thousand have I found; but a woman among all those have I not found."
—ECCLESIASTES

"Among all savage beasts none is found so harmful as woman."
—SAINT JOHN CHRYSOSTOM

"Such is the stupidity of woman's character that it is incumbent upon her in every particular to distrust herself and to obey her husband."

—CONFUCIAN MARRIAGE MANUAL

"If a woman grows weary and at last dies from childbearing, it matters not. Let her only die from bearing, she is there to do it."
—MARTIN LUTHER

"The destiny of woman and her sole glory are to make beat the hearts of man. . . . She is a chattel and properly speaking only a subsidiary of man."

—BALZAC

"I am obnoxious to each carping tongue
Who says my hand a needle better fits . . .
If what I do prove well, it won't advance,
They'll say it's stol'n, or else it was by chance."

—ANNE BRADSTREET

"The presence of a woman would dishonor the Reichstag."

—ADOLF HITLER

The three-hour program was in four parts:

1. A videotape prepared by committeewomen, including sketches in which the women themselves acted, as well as television commercials and children's programs—all designed to illustrate the demeaning way in which the media depict girls and women.

2. A paper presented by a psychologist on the differences in modes of cognition and perception between boys and girls.

3. An informal paper on the image of women in literature.

4. A three-person symposium on women in history.

All four parts of the program were, to some extent, collective efforts—embodying all the hazards, all the liabilities, all the compromises that a collective effort implies, on the one hand, and all of the multi-mind-play enrichment and minimizing of eccentricity on the other. Several of the participants, particularly those with strong political points of view, felt that their individual efforts were somewhat weakened or distorted as a consequence of subordination to group will. Also, many of us have continued to develop and refine a feminist analysis, and, because of evolving political consciousness, would no doubt add to, subtract from, or qualify, what we said at that time. Because, however, the presentation was reflective of group thinking at the time, and because it was effective in terms of raising staff consciousness, I include it here in abbreviated form:

## Extracts from Video Tape.

Ideas and concepts by Mimi Anderson, Cora Lynne David, Donna Barkman, Mimi Meyers, Vivian Ubell; Written and narrated by Donna Barkman; Taped by Cora Lynne David; Technical Assistance by Vivian Ubell and Donna Barkman; Acting by the committee, Leah Matalon and Brett Vuolo.

| VIDEO | AUDIO |
|---|---|
| SHOT OF NORMAN ROCKWELL TRAY (brother and sister eating corn at family table—boy eating gustily, messily; girl prissy, proper, and clean. Slogan at bottom of tray: **Who's having more fun?**) | Well, boys will be boys. We all know what that means, perhaps have even said it ourselves with a shake of the head and a proud, amused gleam in our eyes. We also know what the never-spoken but implicit corollary is: girls will be girls. Forever and ever, we thought. . . . And we thought so long that a few new ideas emerged, chief among them that maybe girls are so identifiably girls, and boys so identifiably boys because we treat them differently. We found that our attitudes were distinctly defined right from the start. If our sons came from the nursery accidentally wrapped in a pink blanket, we were upset; blue for our daughters was not as threatening, although we clearly preferred pink. We recalled that remarks of early admirers also revealed subtle but strong attitudes and expectations based on the baby's sex. |
| BASSINET SKETCH: Sequence of faces looking directly into camera, as if into bassinet. | What is it? A girl? Oh, girls are so much easier than boys. |
| | Hey, Ma, there's a baby in this carriage. What is it, a boy or a girl? Oh, yeah, you can tell it's a boy! Will he be able to play football with me—and baseball? Lookit those muscles. Wow, he's terrific! |
| | Oh, it's a girl . . . well, you can try again. |

SEGUE

We related differently in physical ways to a boy or a girl, starting in their infancy, as illustrated next.

FATHER WITH KIDS (from **Sesame Street**): greets his kids on the street, swings boys in the air, pats girl on head.

HOLD ON SHOT OF SPOCK

We looked to experts, especially Dr. Spock, for advice on everything. He gave it to us and we took it.

(Quote from Spock on relative inherent natures of boys and girls: boys are active, inquisitive, love trucks and taking things apart, etc.; girls are passive, nurturing, compliant—therefore they love to play with dolls, take care of the sick, vote the same as their husbands, and make good "wives, mothers, nurses, and secretaries.")

At this point the audience groaned its way through what appeared to be seventeen-million Barbie-doll-type commercials, and an equal number of odes to floor wax ("I was *proud* of that floor"), table wax, detergents, and toilet-bowl cleansers.

"It goes on forever," whispered one teacher, which was exactly the point. That endless barrage of trivia is what a female television-viewer's life is supposed to be about. The relief that was felt when boy-oriented commercials—boys running, sprinting, astronauting, manipulating trucks and worlds of building equipment—was more expressive of the claustrophobic world girls live in (the message: Boys—the world is yours; Girls—the womb, the kitchen, and the toilet bowl are yours) than any number of words would have been.

| SESAME STREET SEQUENCE of Susan sitting with clothes basket in lap, singing to Bob. | We try to compensate for this barrage [of commercials] by directing our children to better TV. Sesame Street, for instance, offers much that is praiseworthy, but it is not difficult to find sexism rampant in its casting (7 leading male characters, only 1 female— a wife and part-time nurse), and its ever-present depiction of females as beautiful princesses and beautiful mothers. Even when they deliberately show women in varied roles, the focus still seems to be on motherhood as fixed and essential. Never is this done with male role-models. They incessantly imply that fatherhood is secondary to a man, while motherhood is primary to a woman. |
| SESAME STREET SONG with Muppets—two boys and a girl singing **Everyone Likes Ice Cream.** | (Text of song is about likes and dislikes, presumably to show diversity of tastes; however, the "butch" boy likes all tough things, the girl likes adorable things, and the studious-looking boy likes birds and flowers. . . . At the end a word has been blipped.) |
| HOLD ON SHOT OF MUPPETS | "Sissy"—that little boy was called a sissy! The girl is cute and dainty and loves her dolly and is acceptable; the bigger boy is tough and loud and loves his football and is acceptable. The other boy is quiet and loves birds and is called a sissy. Millions of young children have been influenced by this mindless depiction of what little boys and girls are made of. |

SEGUE

SHOTS OF BOOK
ILLUSTRATIONS
SHOWING girls with clasping hands and boys with clenched fists.

We realize that books could be a good source of variety in role portrayals, but there are problems here as well.

One mother spent fifteen minutes surveying her children's books—collections which had been given to, or chosen by her children at random, with no special sexist or nonsexist theories in mind. You are witnessing the portrayal of watching, waiting, fearful girls, and inventive, alert, and adventurous boys. What you are not witnessing is the fact that the girls being shown are almost the only girls to be found; that books about boys (animal or human) are so predominant as to be almost exclusive. The boy child's library: 30 books with boys as title characters—**Babar, Ferdinand the Bull, Rumpelstiltskin, Magilla Gorilla, Winnie the Pooh, Sonny the Lucky Bunny, Joel and the Wild Goose, The Cat in the Hat, Charlie Brown, The Boy at the Dike, Peter Pan, Stuart Little,** et al. And two with girls as star characters: **Snow White** and **The Wizard of Oz.** . . . The girl's library: 18 books chiefly about boys—**The Little Prince, Tom Sawyer, Pinnochio,** Maurice Sendak books, etc., and ten about girls—two **Raggedy Anns,** one ballerina, one doll which comes alive, two **Madelines, Charlotte's Web** (the only nonhuman female-hero in the lot), **Mary Poppins,** and, finally, **Pippi Longstocking.**

SEGUE

We start making assumptions early on, about what will interest girls and boys. We convey these assumptions to them; they mirror them; and we again reinforce. A typical example from this cycle:

CAR SKETCH: Mother trying to drive car in heavy traffic with four very active children demanding attention.

(Mother distracts children by pointing out sights. She alerts boys to tall buildings, cranes, fire trucks, etc. She interests girls in brides and beautiful sunsets. She is then surprised when one boy says, "Girls can't drive school buses.")

HOLD ON SHOT FROM PLEDGE COMMERCIAL of woman dusting piano.

The role models in the home are undeniably one of the most powerful forces in forming a child's picture of what the future holds for her—and him. It is soon apparent that what Daddy does, his work (though not often even viewed by the child), has more importance, more prestige, is more serious than anything Mommy does. This is reiterated in magazines, books, on TV, and all around the neighborhood world of the child.

HOLD ON SHOT OF TWO PEO-PLE reading newspapers held in front of faces.

. . . "Clap hands, clap hands, 'til Daddy comes home, Daddy has money and Mommy has none" goes the chant. This extra weight given to Daddy's existence permeates the entire home atmosphere.

NEWSPAPER SKETCH

(Two people reading newspapers. A child's voice calls "Daddy." A paper shakes a little. "Daddy" again. Same paper quivers.

(Again, "Daddy." Same paper is lowered, to reveal Mommy, who says, "Shush, can't you see your father is reading the paper?")

SHOT OF HANDS turning pages of teen-age girls' magazine showing endless cosmetic and fashion ads.

(Quiet voice-over—comments on hair coloring, makeup, etc.)

They are growing up. Still in the playground, but calling themselves preteens. They are wavering between childhood and adulthood, looking for guidance and rejecting it, trying and testing standards and roles.

While these girls are poring over **Seventeen** and **True Romance** comics and eventually **Glamour** and **June Bride**, their fantasies are focused intensely on fashion and romance, cosmetics and dates, looks, and boys. Their male contemporaries also have magazines specifically directed toward their interests: **Popular Science, Outdoor Life, Hot Rod, Sports Illustrated, Popular Mechanics**—which support boys strongly in their fantasies of adventure, invention, and achievement.

The boy's world is undoubtedly full of pressure to produce and accomplish, but it is nevertheless exciting and expanding. The girl's world is not as stimulating, not as demanding, and is diminishing in its variety of interests.

SHOT OF SMILING SUN

By this point, we have lived with our children closely for a dozen years. But we don't know them.

We don't know them because
they have been obscured by a
murky sexist overlay that has
never allowed them to be viewed
in a clear, pure light. We can't
help them find their truly full potential, because the clouds of
sexual stereotypes have blinded
us all. It's way past time to let the
sun shine in.

A number of schools and institutions asked the Woodward group
to give this presentation for them. The difficulty of working in
collectives is illustrated by this quarrel within the group: the
women working on the video-tape were amateurs. They had
done a very creditable job of editing and working with sophisticated technical equipment, but the seams showed—there were
some "home movie" defects apparent in the finished product.
When, therefore, the group was faced with the prospect of showing the tape to a larger—and possibly less sympathetic—audience, several women who had gained some technical expertise in
the meantime argued strongly for re-doing the tape to make it
more "professional." Others, however, protested that if the tape
were perfect, it would intimidate other women and deter groups
in other schools from undertaking a similar project, because they
might not allow themselves to aspire to a high degree of technical success. The implications of this quarrel are interesting:
"Women won't relate to a slick product" versus "Are we going to
encourage women to remain dilettante, volunteer, homemade-
cookies-for-the-bazaar people forever? Or are we going to show
them that, given the opportunity, women can be every bit as
professional as men? Why should we think women are going to
be intimidated by polished work? Isn't that treating them like
cripples?"

Following the video-tape presentation, Andrea Ostrum, (Ph.D.),
the dedicated feminist who had first publicly raised the issue of
sexism at Woodward, presented the following paper on the psy-

chological development of women. The substance of the talk was derived from two previously published articles: "The Social Construction of the Second Sex" by Jo Freedman, and "Psychology Constructs the Female" by Naomi Weisstein, both of which appear in *Roles Women Play: Readings Towards Women's Liberation* (Ed. Michele Hoffnung Garskoff, Brooks/Cole Publishing Co.).

When we are asked to define the differences between men and women, we get into trouble as soon as we move beyond the most obvious physical factors. And, in fact, we must say that we do not know if there are innate differences between the sexes, or—if there are—what they are. The reason for our state of ignorance is fairly simple to explain. In order to isolate innate differences, one must be able either to go directly to the chromosomes, which at this stage we cannot yet do, or to have access to a society—which does not exist—free of culturally defined sex roles. When we turn to the social sciences for answers, we face an almost insoluble dilemma. Theory gives us creative speculations based on one person's observations and intuition, along with all the accompanying biases—but nothing in the way of scientifically verifiable facts. Research presumes to give us facts, but in truth discounts cultural biases built into the design itself, which almost predetermine the results. For example, a test which is supposed to distinguish between the sexes cannot hope to do so if it is itself contaminated by cultural biases. The behavior of subjects cannot be assumed to reflect sex differences once we know that subjects tend to be influenced by attitudes expressed often nonverbally by the experimenter, and by the behavior of other subjects. For there is nothing in our society about which people are more biased than sex-role stereotypes. Given the choice between faulty research and tenuous theory, one feels a little like facing a choice between Scylla and Charybdis. Having pointed out the pitfalls, however, and having no better alternative, let us turn, always skeptically and tongue-in-cheek, to psychological research and see what we can glean about the development of women in our society.

In the area of intellectual functioning, we find that during pre-school and early elementary years, little girls function on a level superior to that of boys in almost all areas. They speak, read, and count earlier. They have fewer reading and stuttering problems. And, lo and behold, they are even better in math. Once they reach high school, however, a sharp divergence in intellectual functioning begins to appear. By a ⅔ to ⅓ ratio, girls excel in linguistic and verbal areas as opposed to math; while by the same ⅔ to ⅓ ratio, boys excel in math as opposed to verbal areas. When the results of standard achievement tests and school grades are traced over time, we find that the achievement of girls rises, from elementary school until high school, at which point it plummets sharply. The achievement level of boys, however, rises in a slow steady climb from elementary school through high school, cresting in college. What is it that happens along the way? Clearly this difference in pattern cannot be due to innate differences, since, first, girls start out ahead of boys, and, second, there is a sizable deviation from the norm. That ⅓ minority simply cannot be chalked off to genetic exceptions. The other hypothesis left to explore is that the intellectual differences between boys and girls as a group may be affected by differences in the way they are treated socially as they grow up. For us as parents and educators, this is a crucial area to consider.

One factor that has been suggested as affecting intellectual development is early childhood training for independence and problem-solving mastery. Girls are not specifically trained to be dependent, but they are not rewarded or encouraged to be independent the way boys are. Furthermore, the areas in which independence is encouraged are different for the two sexes. Girls seem to be hemmed in by the "safety factor." It is not difficult to imagine little girls being encouraged to go to the store for their mother (close to home), or fixing breakfast for their siblings while parents sleep late. It is more difficult to imagine them being encouraged to venture out in dangerous areas (or farther from home), such as climbing the highest tree, biking out alone, or in later years hitchhiking or traveling alone.

Boys and girls are also raised differently as regards "achievement motivation." Boys are trained to direct and channel their impact on the environment, while girls are protected from the impact of the environment. And contrary to the stereotype of the overprotective, much maligned "mom," fathers are the ones who have been found to play the crucial role in this area. It is they who protect their daughters and push their sons for achievement.

Such differences in childhood training may well be the factors which crucially affect spatial and perceptual organization patterns, which in turn are related to patterning of intellectual development. As early as fourth and fifth grade, boys, having been encouraged to venture out and to explore the outside world, have learned to organize objects in space according to part/whole analysis, an ability necessary for effective mathematical and scientific thinking. Girls of the same age, who have as a rule been held back from active exploration of the environment, tend to organize objects in space according to the gestalt and the surroundings.

Another factor which undoubtedly affects the achievement level of boys and girls is social expectation, or the self-fulfilling prophecy. We are all familiar with the experiment in ghetto schools which proved that those children pointed out to their teachers as "bloomers" did in fact bloom in academic achievement; while those children who were pointed out to their teachers as slow learners lagged in achievement. What probably transpired was that the teachers conveyed their expectations to the children in subtle ways and differentiated in their treatment of them. The children, in turn, conformed to the rewards and punishments handed out to them and to the differences in training.

We must ask ourselves why we are so concerned about the intellectual channeling of our children. Are we saying that girls should be doing whatever boys do? Are not linguistic and verbal abilities and gestalt organizations to be valued as highly as mathematics and science? In the first place, we must recognize that those areas mastered by boys and those traits labeled as male are more highly valued in our society. Male traits and functions are respected and rewarded. And girls are given deficits in "making it" in the world in which we live. Regardless of whether we ourselves accept these values, we must recognize that they do exist and that they will affect our children. Even more important, however, is the fact that social channeling into sex-role stereotypes deprives both boys and girls of freedom of choice. We would be much more comfortable with a 50–50 ratio than with the traditional ⅔–⅓. Finally, girls in our society are faced with an insuperable problem of coping with a socially internalized negative self-image. In social psychology experiments, women have declared that they feel themselves to be "uncertain, anxious, nasty, careless, childish, helpless, timid, stupid, silly, and domestic." They consider themselves blessed with the traits of "understanding, love, affection, tenderness, sympathy, generosity, morality, gratefulness, and patience." Among fourth-graders, ten times as many girls wished they could have been boys as vice versa. Boys of all ages express more preference for the "masculine" role than girls do for the "feminine" role. Among older children asked to vote on who had "good" and "bad" traits, both boys and girls ascribed all the "good" traits to boys. College women, when asked to evaluate essays written by men and women authors, consistently undervalued the essays written by women. The conclusion: conformity to traditional "feminine" behavior, which is rewarded for girls, is accompanied by barriers to achievement and by self-devaluation.

In addition, girls are presented with a double bind. Not only must they worry about failure, but also about success. For a woman to succeed in our society means renouncing many of the so-called "feminine" traits which have been held out to her, and incorporating many traits which in our society have been labeled as "masculine." Women are therefore forced to make a choice that no one should have to make. To be fully "feminine" almost guarantees being unsuccessful. To be successful means at least in part being "masculine" as things have been defined for us since birth. Many women opt against success. Others attempt the solution I call the "superwoman syndrome." They "make it" outside, and then come home to be super-mother, super-housekeeper (or housekeeper supervisor), and of course super-cook. Now there is nothing wrong with any of those things. It is just a terrible burden for anyone to feel she has to be all of them.

The bind women find themselves in was, I think, best put by the successful writer Ann Burstein. She said that what troubled her most was not the struggle to succeed against heavy odds, but rather the psychic cost of being a woman. No matter how great her success, she said, in some small corner of her mind, part of her was still arguing the case. What couldn't all that emotion and energy have accomplished if it was not directed into perpetually arguing the case for success? If she were a man, and freed from that burden, she continued, she was sure she could have soared. As a woman, her wings were clipped. We—parents and teachers—must work together for our girls to grow into free, independent, self-loving persons, without having their wings clipped in the process.

Andrea's paper was followed by a collective paper on women in history, compiled and presented by Carol London, Brett Vuolo, and Adrienne Yurick.

Pythagoras says, "There is a good principle which created order, light, and man, and an evil principle, which created chaos, darkness, and woman."

Aristotle says, "We may thus conclude that it is a general law that there should be naturally ruling elements and elements naturally ruled . . . the rule of the freeman over the slave in one kind of rule; that of the male over the female another . . . the slave is entirely without the faculty of deliberation; the female indeed possesses it, but in a form that remains inconclusive."

According to German scientist P. J. Moebius, "If the feminine abilities were developed to the same degree as those of the male, her maternal organs would suffer and we should have a repulsive and useless hybrid."

Historian Arthur M. Schlesinger says, "An examination of the standard histories of the United States and of most of the history textbooks in use in our schools raises the pertinent question whether women have ever made any contributions to American national progress that are worthy of record. If the silence of our historians is to mean anything, it would appear that one-half of our population have been negligible factors in our country's history."

Silence indeed! We began to work on this presentation with the notion that the role of women had been neglected in our history books. What we found in our search was even more amazing than we expected. Women are all but invisible in the books from which we all learned our history. We have examined many history texts—texts that we all might have encountered in high school and college—as well as books published within the last ten years. We have found that women just don't seem to be part of American history. Here are a few examples: Henry Steele Commager's **Documents of American History** (1962), a compilation of 665 documents, includes four by or about women. **A Documentary History of the American People** (Craven, Johnson and Dunn, 1951), a Columbia University text, contains 238 documents—three by or about women! **The Oxford History of the American People,** by Samuel Eliot Morrison (1965), sums up the role of women in colonial times in four lines! Mr. Morrison also sees fit to place his two lines covering the Nineteenth Amendment under the heading "Bootlegging and Other Sports."

*"On the basis of the information in these commonly used texts, one might summarize the history and contributions of the American woman as follows: Women arrived in 1619. They held the Seneca Falls Convention on Women's Rights in 1848. During the rest of the nineteenth century they participated in reform movements, chiefly temperance, and were exploited in factories. In 1923, they were given the vote. They joined the armed forces for the first time during the Second World War, and thereafter have enjoyed the good life in America. In those texts which did include women in one area or another, we found a pattern of inclusions and neglects that presented a stereotyped picture

* Trecker, Janice Law "Women in U.S. History High School Tests," **Report on Sex Bias in the Public Schools** (New York: National Organization for Women, 1971).

of the American woman—passive, incapable of sustained work or organization, satisfied with her role in society and well equipped with material blessings."

Where are Phyliss Wheately and Anne Bradstreet, America's first professional poets? Where are Prudence Crandall and Myrtilla Miner, stoned, bombed, and persecuted for being the first to set up schools for black girls? Where are Ida B. Wells and MaryAnn Shadd Carey, crusading black newspaper editors? Where are Sarah Bagley and Mary Harris Jones, leaders in the labor unions? Does the simple phrase, "Women were given the vote" even hint at the struggle which cost American women, in the words of Carrie Chapman Catt, "52 years of pauseless campaign; 56 state referendum campaigns; 480 legislative campaigns to get state suffrage amendments submitted; 47 state constitutional convention campaigns; 277 state party convention campaigns; 30 national party convention campaigns to get suffrage planks in the party platforms; 19 campaigns with 19 successive Congresses to get the federal amendment submitted, and the final ratification campaign"? Does the statement that some "educational opportunities for women improved in the nineteenth century" really do justice to the fact that women had literally to fight their way into colleges and universities and that they surmounted enormous obstacles to found schools and colleges for themselves? Can the social conditions that drove women into the Temperance Movement be reduced to a humorous description of the antics of Carrie Nation? What about Dr. Elizabeth Blackwell, Emma Willard, Abigail Scott Duniway, Dr. Anna Howard Shaw, Mary Lyon, Lucy Stone, Charlotte Forten, the Grimké sisters? We need to know about these women, not only what they accomplished, but what they had to struggle against in order to accomplish it.

What were those millions of faceless American women doing at any given point in our history? What conditions were they living under? What were their struggles to survive, to change the conditions of their lives?

It has been said that women's diaries, journals and letters are their "literature." We need to dig up these primary sources to find out how women lived and what they felt and thought and did—or couldn't do. We need to know about women on plantations, on the lonely farms, in factories, schools, and labor unions, in order to reclaim our past from obscurity and in order to understand our present.

Our purpose here is not to tell you how to teach history, but to try to show how our own history has been hidden from us, depriving us all—men as well as women, parents as well as teachers—of a sense of ourselves in history. (Brett Vuolo)

One of the political differences which was much discussed within the group, was whether, in fact, it was a distortion of historical process to see it in terms of heroes and heroines. The exponents of this point of view argued that we shouldn't need to have either heroes or heroines, that our history books are already too full of Big Names (history, they felt, was not the lengthened shadow of a man *or* a woman; to see it that way was to ignore social, economic, and political process). To this, Brett Vuolo, who prepared the foregoing part of the history presentation, says: "When I hear that, my instinctive response is, 'Give us our heroines and we'll give them up when we're good and ready!' I *want* my daughter to know about women who struggled to do what they wanted to do, and succeeded. But I also want her to know about the millions of women who struggled ineffectually, and why their struggle was futile." She adds, "We do need to look at history in a new light—a light that shows us what the people were doing behind the scenes while all those generals, statesmen, and inventors were parading across the stage." What is implicit in this argument is the necessity for feminists to define what they mean by "success." Is any strong, goal-oriented, achieving woman to be judged a success and offered to our children as a role model? Would a four-star woman general in the United States Army be a success, because she has scaled heights previously unattained by women in a man's field? Or do we judge her also by the institution which she serves? Some feminist writers have suggested that "we must rejoice indiscriminately in the achievement of economically and professionally successful women," because not to do so reveals a pathological fear of power; one public feminist—a psychologist—implies that to make a judgment that "Caesar's power" or the institutions of Caesar are not worthy of aspiring to springs from "the female belief that she cannot be enhanced or protected by the success or power of any other women."

If that is so, then women will all be obliged to rejoice when the CIA is staffed with high-ranking women. Can this really be so? Is a successful woman a woman who gets her share of the pie if the pie is crawling with maggots? Does one rejoice equally for a conservative woman and a socialist woman elected to the legislature? Does one say *brava* with equal fervor to Angela Davis and to Elizabeth I, to a poet and a corporation president? To know what kinds of role models are worth having, we must decide what kind of "success" is worth having, and again we are faced with the necessity of making a political–moral analysis (a necessity that is particularly onerous to me, because I tend to be attracted to or repelled by people idiosyncratically, by their style—as good a way as any, perhaps, to choose pleasant companions and amusing company, but not the sanest way to go about selecting heroines or role models, if that is what one is about).

A consideration of the organic relationship between the abolition movement and the women's rights movement provides a good example of what we mean by history as **process.** In order to understand our history, we need to search for information about the social and cultural roles and attitudes which determined the way people lived; and we need to know the private and public, legal, and religious status of various groupings of people. We need to know how people earned or did not earn their livings; how they functioned at home or at work. In order to understand the abolition movement and the Women's Rights Movement, we need to know what forces developed to enable these Movements to grow. We need to examine the conditions under which white women, freed blacks, rich men and women, Northern and Southern, lived and struggled to survive and to effect change. We must regard history as social, political, and economic process, and not a succession of battles, heroes, and significant speeches.

In order to understand the abolition movement, it is essential to know the conditions under which black slaves lived; the differences, for example, between the male slave and the female slave: the female black slave, because she was a breeder and a nurturer of more slaves, was the recognized "head" of her family. Since males were readily bought and sold, the black woman was not subjected to masculine authority as such, but was, rather, a victim of sexual assault by white owners and overseers. The myth of endangered Southern womanhood was used as a basis for slavery. Poor and rich white women alike had to be protected and kept from violating any conventions, because they were presumably in danger of attack by the sexually brutal black male.

It is equally important to understand what the battle over slavery was about, economically and politically: it was a battle for power between two economic systems—plantation versus industry, field-worker versus cheap labor, and agriculture versus capital investment.

We hear too little about the restrictive laws against black people in those very Northern states that encouraged runaway slaves to settle there; too little about the funding of black settlers by rich industrialists and plantation owners, who armed and manipulated people to fight for "free soil" or "slave state" without concern for the slaves themselves. We hear too much about the noble aims of Lincoln (who was mistrusted by abolitionists) and of the speeches of Calhoun and Webster . . . too much, that is to say, of the morality of the north and the ignobility of the south.

The process of struggling against slavery brought black and white women together in the underground railroad, in antislavery societies and conventions. Such women as Charlotte Forten, Sarah Redmond, the Grimké sisters, Lucy Stone, Harriette Tubman, and many, many more were essential to the abolition movement, but their work goes largely unnoticed in comparison to that of the "important men."

The process of organizing against slavery brought to women an acute understanding of their position as women. It was within this movement that the struggle for human emancipation of black people and of women became cogent and liberating forces. The restrictions preventing women from speaking publicly about slavery led them to speak and write about their own rights. The realization that most male abolitionists did not think their cause justified led women to organize their own organizations.

The abolition movement, as well as the Women's Rights Movement, rose in the industrial North, where their employment outside the home made women more independent than women in the sheltered homes of the South. The growing industrialization of the North during the mid-nineteenth century was accompanied by the constant turmoil of radical beliefs and labor agitation. By 1850, women constituted 24 percent of the labor force. They had no rights, legal or moral, to personhood. They worked under hideous conditions and went home to do all the work in their households after working from twelve to fifteen hours for less pay than men. They went on strikes and held demonstrations, but they lacked organization. The movement for abolition gave women the experience of organizing. At the same time, schools were being set up for more children than ever before—not entirely for humanitarian reasons; schools served to remove children from family interests and make them more available to business interests. This applied less to girls, especially older ones, and women like Mary Lyon did the work of enabling women to have the benefits of intellectual training. Schools for black girls developed, but went under, unable to survive against the strong pressures brought to bear against them. The opening of the West during this time and the call of the growing cities made girls more defiant of parental authority, giving them a greater desire to choose their own work.

Internal divisions among the Quakers—about orthodoxy and "the inner light"—which women participated in, helped women to demand equality. The various religious doctrines which had been used to keep women in subjugation were being questioned by women, especially the Quaker women, who led the abolition movement. The ferment of intellectual and political questioning taking place at that time caused women to question their own roles and their place in society.

These were some of the underlying conditions giving rise to the growth of the dual movements: abolition, and women's rights. The information regarding both is hard to come by but necessary to find, if we are to understand our history. (Adrienne Yurick)

This paper did not deal with the painful schisms that arose within the Women's Rights Movement: When Sojourner Truth made her heart-rending cry, "And ain't I a woman?" she was addressing herself to white women, some of whom were not sure they wanted to include black women in the struggle for equal rights. The suffrage movement was also rent by quarrels over "priorities": Many white women felt that their getting the vote should take precedence over the black man's getting the vote. The coalition between the two dual movements was not an easy one. A serious study of the abolition and Women's Rights Movements ought to illuminate these difficulties and divergences, some of which may have application to our own struggles today.

Sometimes, for want of any other historical data, literature provides the only clues to the way people lived. Because there is so little written about the actual lives of pioneer women, it is enlightening to consider the life of one woman—Beret, in America's first psychological novel, O. E. Rolvaag's **Giants in the Earth**—as a representative of pioneer women in general. Recently discovered diaries of pioneer women suggest that Beret was not atypical.

Per Hansa, his very pregnant wife, Beret, and their three children had left Norway for the vast and virgin plains of the Dakota territory, plains so untrampled even the grass rejected the invasion by people, moaning Tish'a, Tish'a with each of their steps.

Journeying to her new home on the barren and desolate plains,

Beret Hansa had almost immediate misgivings. "This seems to be taking us to the end of the world . . . beyond the end of the world." But her fears and concerns were never openly acknowledged, for she "wept silently" and rarely complained. Per, the "natural pioneer," eagerly looked upon approaching darkness as the signal that a new and even more exciting day was soon to come—a day with the potential for challenge and for new adventures. For Beret, anxiety was the accompaniment of each approaching night. She dreaded it and saw only more blackness in an accumulation of bleak days and even bleaker nights.

While her husband considered the wilderness an exciting challenge to his creativity, "Beret considered it to be a place where human beings could not endure. And she had so many fears and had experienced so much loneliness that she could not share." She had lived for six weeks and more without seeing another civilized face. "Not a settled habitation of man lay nearer than several days' journey; if any visitor came, it was a savage, a wild man, whom one must fear. . . . What would happen if something sudden should befall them—attack, sickness, fire, etc.? And then what of the children? They would grow up to be like the savages."

And yet Beret came willingly because there were no other options for her. It was a matter of course that a woman would go wherever her husband led her. Per Hansa "loved" her, yet he treated her as a child. He wanted her to share his life, but he tried to prevent her from knowing about its intense and necessary unpleasantness.

Because of a broken wagon, Per Hansa and his family had to stay behind the other families with whom they had originally set out. When Per realized that they had become quite lost in the vastness, he did not consider telling his wife for fear of frightening her. But she sensed that something was wrong; her lack of knowledge promulgated a fear far greater than the reality of being lost would have done. Beret suffered as a result of ignorance until, frustrated beyond silence, she burst into tears which Per Hansa paternally tried to calm by patting her and calling her "Beret Girl." To make her feel better and to satisfy what he evidently thought was sexual need, he did what he considered appropriate to the situation—"That night Per Hansa was good to his wife."

When there was a problem with land claims, Per Hansa did not consider discussing this with Beret. He kept her at a distance, since it was not believed that women could deal with such "manly," worldly concerns. He would not mention his anxiety and fear; thus the real problem was intensified. He felt deserted and alone, but he did not consider consulting and sharing his concerns with his wife. Beret was filled with a gnawing loneliness. She, who longed for friends, began to seem so queer that people didn't visit her. And, instead of discussing the causes, Per Hansa paternally told her to comb her hair, and made her feel ashamed of her slovenly appearance. She was acting like a normal, but terribly frightened, human being.

The vastness of empty blocks of time encouraged flights from reality. Beret had left the comfortable civilization of Norway, a comfortable house, close family, and friends, for her husband's dream—which for her was just a house made of sod. She left the comfort of stitching a sampler in front of a warm fire for a wilderness where not only was there no privacy in general, but "there was nothing to hide behind." She had left friends and family for a "prairie that had no heart that beat, no waves that sang, no soul that could be touched. . . ." She truly expected her husband to realize that they must go back "to the place where human beings dwelt." Only they never talked about how they felt; this was not the stuff of communication between man and woman.

When Beret timidly expressed her fear of the openness and emptiness, the absence of other human beings, her husband did not acknowledge the reasonableness of her concerns. Instead, "he laughed so long and loud, she winced at it." He called her "girl" and told her, as one would a child, "Never you fear." He talked about the wilderness being "their kingdom," which he would "rule." But he could never "make" her understand because "she was not built to wrestle with fortune."

But this "girl" of Per Hansa's was pregnant and expected to "bear the brunt of it"—bringing up children, cooking, cleaning, and whatever else "the woman usually does." And Per Hansa did understand that Beret was "a woman of tender kindness, of deep, fine fancies—one whom you could not treat like an ordinary clod." This gentle, fine woman, who had been successfully bred for Norwegian society, did try to support her husband physically as well as emotionally; that was her role. Per Hansa went out to the fields to till the land, and when the job required additional hands, Beret joined the men and "took her full term like any man." Except that she also had to attend to her little daughter who had to accompany her to the fields. In addition to her child-care responsibilities, she returned from the fields, pregnant and sore, only to give the men their evening meal.

Beret left the safety and security of her homeland as a result of her love for her husband. Most women left for similar reasons. Some left because of duty. "Whither thou goest, I will go" was deeply a part of the psyches of women. And Per Hansa seemed predestined to become a pioneer. Since Beret could not adopt a similar enthusiasm, she not only longed for the past, she considered herself a hindrance to the future—and to Per Hansa—"like chains around his feet; him, whom she loved unto madness, she burdened and impeded."

And so Beret, and many others like her, were contradictions to the myth of the robust pioneering woman. Other Berets went insane as she did. She went to America "out of love." What else could a woman do? Her entire existence was tied up with her man and her children. But, on the other hand, most men—and this included Per Hansa—had been permitted if not encouraged to grow up with the idea that adventure in life was a real possibility. The women had been taught domestic tasks that were centered around their comfortable little homes. But the floor-scrubbing, vegetable-cooking, and Bible-reading were inadequate preparations for a wilderness life. The pioneer woman couldn't gossip over the fence because there was no fence and neighbors were far apart. Parents and most friends were still "back home." Women were treated as if they were children. Problems were never discussed with them—the world was planned for them. They didn't share the problems of the men, but were left to wonder and to despair.

(Carol London)

The history presentation was followed by my paper on the image of women in literature. Many of the concepts, and a few of the examples outlined in it are derived from *The Second Sex*, by Simone de Beauvoir.

To begin at the beginning: Cinderella waits for Prince Charming. She waits for him to rescue her—from other women. Fairy tales establish the pattern: Women wait. Women are needy. Women need protectors—male protectors. Women are in competition with other women for the man who will make them complete. There are no evil stepfathers in fairy tales. There are no warlocks who dangle curses over cradles. In fairytales, women are either Beautiful Princesses, Evil Stepmothers, or Witches. Terrible, mysterious, primeval powers are ascribed to women, but God help the contemporary woman who is straightforward, or foolish enough to demand power right up front—then she is no longer "womanly."

Women in love recognize themselves in Hans Christian Andersen's little mermaid—the one who exchanged her fishtail for legs because of love and had, thereafter, to walk on knives and live coals. Her love was a need so great she was willing to sacrifice her entire essence, literally to give herself away. It turned out, of course, that "he" didn't want her anyway.

It may be argued that man's need is equally great. But we don't find, in literature, men who are both needy and passive. Men do great deeds for love. Women wait. Rapunzel waited in her tower. Henry James's heroines await rescue from the consequences of their headstrong romanticism. ("Headstrong," incidentally, is a word seldom applied to men. That's what they're supposed to be.) Women seldom initiate aggressive action; they do, of course, manipulate, and they are devious. And they suffer mightily for it—they don't get their man.

The energy that men give to their art and to their work, needy women give to love. Try to imagine a woman saying, "I could not love thee dear so much loved I not honour more." Joan of Arc might have said it, but we all know what happened to her. The word "honor" is seldom applied to women. When a woman, in books, is described as honorable, noble, or faithful, what is usually meant is that she is sexually true to her man. Men are faithful to their ideals, to themselves, or to their countries—and seldom to their women.

When, in Ibsen's **Doll House**, Nora's husband, Helmer, says: "Only lean on me, let me counsel and guide you, I wouldn't be a true man if this very womanly helplessness didn't make you doubly attractive in my eyes," he is giving perfect expression to the belief that women—frail, helpless, childish, and charming—need protectors and mentors.

Recently, in France—in a case that became as notorious as the Dreyfus case—a woman established herself as a young man's mentor. Gabrielle Rousseau, a thirty-year-old teacher, had a love affair with a seventeen-year-old student (who was, in fact, the aggressor: he initiated the relationship by breaking her door down). She was brought to trial for having corrupted (or, according to the French, "deviated") the morals of a child. The French, of course, have a literary tradition of older women sexually initiating younger men, but Rousseau—as the French press pointed out—made the mistake of confusing literature with real life. She paid for her mistake with her life. While it is inconceivable that a man would have been so prosecuted—or persecuted—for the "crime" of having sexual relationships with a consenting young woman, the French trotted out provisions in the law that had gone unused for one hundred years. Gabrielle Rousseau—her career ruined—killed herself. Whereupon the French immediately began to write essays. The French male Left, incredibly, read into this affair a morality lesson on the differences between Maoism and Communism; evidently a woman's personal pain was not judged worthy enough, or interesting enough, to be the subject of learned debate.

We learn, from literature, that women need mentors. We also learn that they need to be tamed. "A little wholesome brutality" is thought to be good for a woman. The stronger, the more rebellious a woman, the greater her need for male dominance. Which brings us to the confusing, conflicting lessons girls learn from literature: we learn that it is good to be strong; but that it is in our best interest to be weak . . . better still—as Simone de Beauvoir has pointed out—to be weak and vapid; best of all to be weak, vapid, and blonde. Literature is full of independent, rebellious girls who long to sacrifice their pride to a man. What else would a girl do with her independence but surrender it? The young girl who opposes the world is touching, says de Beauvoir; but the world is too strong; if she persists in her opposition, it breaks her. Too much daring, culture, intelligence, or character frightens men; in most novels, as George Eliot remarks, it is the blond and silly heroine who is victorious over the less feminine brunette.

In **Pride and Prejudice**, Jane Austen created a heroine, Elizabeth Bennet, who was independent, witty, sensible, gay, intelligent, kind, vital, good, and brunette. She was fortunate to find a man like Darcy to shelter her. In a later novel—not a very good one—Jane Austen created a heroine who was the antithesis of Elizabeth. Fanny, the heroine of **Mansfield Park**, has no energy, she is a shy intruding angel; she is forever "grateful" to the man she loves (a boring prig); she is blonde; and she is victorious—for the love of the prig—over a competitor whose only crime is vitality and wit. One wonders what Jane Austen (who never married) was taught by the world, between those two novels.

Conflicting messages are also sent out by **Little Women.** Probably everyone will agree that tomboy Jo is the most attractive of the girls. But Jo, who deifies her heroic, absent father, spends all her time trying to be what he wants her to be—that is, a "little woman," a stereotypically feminine woman. It is true that Jo turns down the little rich boy, Laurie, who wants to marry her, but certainly the message received by the reader is that if you want to marry somebody rich and handsome, you'd better be blonde and silly like Amy. Jo was fit only to be Laurie's childhood playmate. His mature love was reserved for feminine Amy. (Girls who don't get dates usually identify with Jo.) Again, the message is: blondes have more fun. Louisa May Alcott never married either.

I'll pass over the depiction of prostitutes in literature, although it is wonderful how even such great writers as Dostoevsky assume that a prostitute is better than a confessional . . . telling a prostitute your worst sins seems to put you automatically in a state of grace.

Women are often glorified in art. In literature they are nurturing, sustaining, loving, patient, economical, generous, practical, and giving. Why would anyone object to that?

A prime example of this kind of idealizing of women—in fact the winner of the earth-mother sweepstakes—is **Grapes of Wrath**. When I reread this book I was struck by the number of times I saw this sentence: **The women stood silently and watched. And the women stood and waited.** (Dorothy Parker said the same thing, with a slightly different emphasis: "All your life you wait for some damn man.") In **Grapes of Wrath**, ma is the character we love and remember. She is described as "the citadel of the family . . . the strong place that could not be taken." But, "And the women came out of their houses to stand beside their men to feel whether this time the men would break . . . the women studied the men's faces secretly; then the women knew that they were safe. . . . The women went into their houses to their work. The men sat still, thinking, figuring." That recurring image of the women watching the men's faces as barometers of their fate is pathetic. Steinbeck gives women credit for greater flexibility than men: He says, "Women can change better than a man. Woman got all her life in her arms. Man got it all in his head." (Obviously you can't have a head and a heart too.)

Steinbeck has women buttoning up grown men's shirts. He has his women protecting grown men against the consequences of their own emotions, while men "protect" women from the world. Men's emotions are strangers to them: "Don't go near your father," ma says to her son. "He might whale you if you go near him. She knew that a man so hurt and perplexed may turn in anger, even on people he loves." Ma never turns on the people she loves.

What do Steinbeck's women get for all this supposed superiority? What do they get for mediating between man and his emotions, between man and the world? Well, for one thing, they don't get to "think and figure"—that's for men to do. The façade of male superiority has to be kept up at all costs. What Steinbeck is saying is: we know you're stronger than we are, but keep your place; we'll make the decisions. You may have the power; we have the authority. The social game has to be played.

Men die violent and bitter deaths in **Grapes of Wrath**, sometimes noble deaths. They die for a cause. Women are involved in one physical battle: in a tent city they throw garbage at one another. And of course the men, amused, protect the women from one another. So these "citadels" of strength are just silly, contentious women after all.

What else do women get for being so loving and so strong? Well, Casey the preacher says, "When a woman is so great with love she scares me. Makes me afraid and mean." You can't win. The message is: we want your love, we want your support, we want your strength, but be forewarned; we're not up to it, it'll scare us and make us mean.

Ma welcomes her husband's meanness. She says, "He ain't beat. He's like as not to take a smack at me." There's the notion of a little wholesome brutality again. She measures her husband's strength in direct ratio to how much he oppresses her.

There's a lot about pregnancy and childbirth in **Grapes of Wrath.** Every male is always going on about the proud and fearful mysteries of childbirth. Rose of Sharon is pregnant. What does it get her? Well, what it doesn't get her is a seat in the car. She has to stand up because she's young and because she's a woman. It's like being a black in Faulkner's South—a black is more noble, more compassionate, more spiritual than a white, but a black has to sit down in the back of the bus. The awe that Steinbeck's men speak of, in relation to pregnancy, seems to me to be another aspect of their contempt. Steinbeck speaks of pregnant Rose of Sharon smiling a "wise smile, her mouth tipped at the corners a little fatuously." Anyone who thinks it's possible to smile wisely and fatuously at the same time must surely be suffering some degree of ambivalence.

The real tear-jerker in **Grapes of Wrath** is the final scene: Rose of Sharon, her baby aborted, offers the milk of her breast to a starving man. It is a selfless act, combining the best qualities of earth-mother and goddess . . . and no woman could have written it. Only a man could write that with a straight face. A woman would have been too aware of the ironies implicit in that final giving.

Women reject the privileged role of earth-mother in art. From earth-mother to "Jewish mother" to all-American bitch is an easy progression. It is a progression American novelists have found it extremely easy to make.

In **A Room of One's Own,** Virginia Woolf contrasts the life of an imaginary sister of Shakespeare with his life of learning and adventure. Whatever became of Shakespeare's sister, she asks? And what was Mrs. Portnoy's complaint, we might add? When women begin to find a psychic room of their own, when they refuse to exist merely as the subject-matter of art, they will have the answers.

After we read our papers, staff and sex-roles committeewomen sat around in a circle and talked easily and without pressure. We talked about the *how* of our children's liberation from the bondage of sex roles, not the *why*. It was obvious that changes had been wrought in the staff's consciousness. The response from the female staff members was particularly heartening. A flood of confirming anecdotes—where we had anticipated defense, agitation, disagreement—was released. The work of the Sex-roles Committee in earnest, organized form, had begun in September, 1970. We had been called then "Women's Lib freaks," and "inside agitators." Somehow, over the past months, the staff's attitude toward us had changed. Many staff members were now, by all indications, inclined to look upon us as partners rather than as nuisances—or at least as sober women whose concerns had also to be the school's concerns. Exactly how much this change in attitude was due to our pressuring and our efforts at consciousness-raising, and how much it was due to public acceptance of feminist demands in the general consciousness, it was hard to say. Several staff members had, in the nine months that we had been functioning as a committee, joined their own consciousness-raising groups. This did not necessarily make them amenable to all our requests and demands—the reality of their being part of an institution undergoing pressure from a group not always, as they saw it, sensitive to their own necessities as teachers and members of a staff faced with the necessity of making cooperative decisions, still existed.

I don't mean to imply that everybody at that meeting was in love with us: one woman teacher, irritated by what she apparently considered the belaboring of the obvious during the videotape presentation, left unceremoniously; one male teacher absented himself altogether. In general, however, we felt that we, and our message, had been accepted. The tone of the meeting was good natured and relaxed; we felt charitable toward one another; no one assumed ill-will of anyone else; the meeting did not have the feel of a confrontation between opposition forces.

Sex-roles committeewomen were conscious of another kind of victory at that meeting. For long months, a diverse group of feminists—women who shared no political ideology, whose perceptions, opinions, and ideals were often sharply at variance with one another's—had met communally, in order to make changes in an institution each perceived differently. The victory that gave us the most pleasure that fine June day was the feeling of solidarity within the group, the feeling of love for one another, our collective recognition that we had worked hard together in a good cause, surviving disputations without rancor and animosity. We had surprisingly often been able to subordinate our differences to the love for our daughters and our sons which we had in common; we had formed a working union, which, however imperfect, had produced radical change. We liked one another a lot. We still do. Most of us look back at that year, and say, *It was good.* We continue to grow, to change, and to disagree; but many strong friendships came out of our group, and many of us learned what "sisterhood" really means.

At the June meeting, there were two demurrals from consensus that I remember: one teacher argued that our older, teen-age children were "there—liberated—already." In the general discussion of whether teen-age boys and girls were liberating themselves from stereotypical sex roles, the "boys cook at barbecues; girls hitchike" syndrome, an anecdote Andrea Ostrum told stands out in my mind: Andrea had been arrested at the Washington May Day demonstrations; in her jail cell, the imprisoned young women chanted FREE OUR BROTHERS. Nobody heard, or expected to hear, an answering FREE OUR SISTERS from the male cell.

Another teacher said, "Most of the women here are parents of younger children. Before the school commits itself to a liberationist point of view, we should get the agreement of parents of older children."

"We didn't wait till we got the agreement of every parent for a Black Studies program," said Marge Hammock, the one black woman present, "and we're not going to wait till they all say it's OK for Woodward to have nonsexist education."

"We were integrated before most other schools were," added Gertrude Goldstein, "and we didn't ask the parents' permission to integrate. Some of our parents still have doubts and complaints because we don't push their first-graders to read and write. Some parents don't like interaging. We act on the best evidence available to us and we are committed to what we think is right for our children. We hope we can carry the minority of protesting parents along when they see the results."

Sex-roles committeewomen took that for a commitment.

We talked about ways for this commitment to be translated into action: feminists agreed to continue to work at providing materials to supplement and enrich the curriculum, and to provide the school with outside resource people—invited at the school's discretion—who would be strong, positive role models; we mutually agreed to consider a feminist elective for upper grades; one which would be staffed by feminist volunteers. We talked, too, about taping oral histories of women, a collaborative venture in which black and white women could share with good heart.

Whether any, or all of these projects would work, of course, would depend on whether unconscious attitudes toward boys and girls had really changed, on the degree of feminist commitment after the initial surge of energy, and on the depth of the school's commitment to nonsexist education.

At the beginning of the 1971–1972 school year, exactly a year after the Sex-roles Committee had began its work, parents received this letter from Ms. Goldstein:

> In the study of man's development at all levels we plan to be increasingly aware of the contributions of groups long overlooked. This includes the vast contributions of the entire non-Western, non-white, non-Christian world.
>
> Attention also needs to be focused on the changing roles of women and men and the part that women have played in building our civilization.

If the consciousness of the school had not been raised sufficiently for Gertrude to realize that *human* development might—in the context of that letter—have been more appropriate than *man's* development, feminists could at least be happy that our concerns—dismissed a year before as "fringe interests"—were now officially regarded as part of school policy.

# 9

# Changes, 1971-1972

This is the fourth time today
you've said "Women's Lib."
—FOURTH-GRADE STUDENT

In the summer of 1970, many Woodward women were beginning
to become actively involved in the women's Movement. By the
summer of 1971, many of them were making decisions about
their lives, based on the insights and impetus gained from a year's
consciousness-raising. By the fall of 1971, when school began
again, many of the women most active in the Sex-roles Committee
had gone back to school or to jobs; most were busy, one way or
another, scraping the metaphorical rust away from their lives,
and more actively participating in the work of the world. The
Sex-roles Committee continued to function, but without the same
thrust and intensity that had dynamized the group the year before.

The committee presented programs to the parent body, the
PTA, and upper-grade students; it made more connections with
upper-grade teachers, and gave more thought to the problems of
Woodward's older children, who had been somewhat disre-
garded in the blocks-and-dolls discussions of the early days of the
committee.

I do not claim to have any insight into the psyches of pre-teenage
children, who are a mystery to everybody, themselves included.
They are so volatile that they defy any attempt at definition or
categorization; they swing wildly from supersophistication ( *The*

*Sensuous Woman* was practically the Bible of seventh- and eighth-grade girls in 1971) to childishness (the very mention of "sex roles" was often enough to send the girls—who were beginning to read sexual innuendos into everything—into paroxysms of giggles. (One teacher who was so unfortunate as to use the phrase "social intercourse" was unable to calm her class down for ten minutes.) When the Feminist Book Collective presented its slide show to upper graders, they reacted with embarrassment and cynicism, as if it were irrelevant to them; they already knew, they said, that women could work outside the home—their mothers worked, *so what?* And the reason so many women are secretaries, they said, is that "Men don't want to be secretaries, women *do*."

Seventh- and eighth-grade girls are beginning to dissimulate; afraid of competing, they are inclined to hide their aptitudes. To say this is not to ignore the fact that boys have their own problems; to begin to be aware of the burdens they will have to assume as men can't be other than overwhelming.

One seventh-grade class was asked, as an English assignment, to create a fictitious person and describe his or her life. Several girls chose to write about males, but not one boy wrote about a female. One bright adventurous girl projected a picture of a woman not unlike herself, who, after a dazzling college experience, married, had children when she was twenty-two, twenty-four, and twenty-eight, and died—nothing at all having happened to her after the birth of her last child—at the age of seventy. An emptiness between twenty-eight and seventy, between childbirth and death. . . . Ironically, the mother of the girl who wrote this fictional portrait is a professional working woman. It would be unthinkable, of course, to write about a man in similar terms. It's amazing how invisible women are.

According to their teachers, children of this age are hypersensitive one minute, gross (one of their favorite words) the next. They are—their teachers say—beginning to be troubled by their perceptions of ambiguities and paradoxes. The world and people no longer seem to them to be black and white, good and bad. They are learning that conflicts do not always lend themselves to ready solution by benign authorities. It's difficult for them to step outside themselves and look objectively at their socialization;

they're beginning to be interested in sex; they are not aware of and certainly don't want to be told what psychological influences have been brought to bear upon them to mold them into sexual, role-playing beings. On the other hand, Gaila Coughlin, a seventh-grade teacher, reported that they were very curious about *her* sexuality. The girls in her class frequently asked her, she says, "Would you be willing to get married again? Would you be willing to look again?" They were asking her if she had a man, or if she was turned off by men and sex, in which case, they obviously felt she would find it impossible to understand them.

Girls this age—again my information comes from their teachers—hate lectures and being boringly lectured to; they resent being hit on the head with adult value judgments and abstractions. Their teachers feel they learn best in small, protected groups where they don't feel visible, vulnerable, self-conscious, and called upon to play appropriate roles—and to giggle at the mention of sex.

These perceptions of upper-grade teachers led sex-roles committeewomen and staff members to the conclusion that electives for seventh- and eighth-grade girls might be the best way to raise their consciousness about sex roles. The elective might, for example, include a study of "girls and their bodies"; it might also, inasmuch as girls of this age are so much interested in fashion, include a study of how clothing and the advertising of it reflects cultural and societal mores. It was felt that role models were particularly useful as an adjunct for study for the upper grades—women and men who are engaged in nonstereotypical endeavors make points more palatably than the abstractions these kids tend to reject or rebel against. Upper-grade teachers and Sex-roles Committee members also decided to invite upper-grade children to a Sex-roles Committee meeting—to satisfy the kids' curiosity about "what was going on."

So during the 1971–1972 school year, while sex-roles committeewomen continued to supply the school with materials, compile bibliographies, and prepare files of resource people, we did nothing very dramatic, we undertook no major projects. Our attitude was one of hopeful expectancy.

It had gotten about, in the meantime, that feminist activity at Woodward had produced changes; the committee and the staff were approached by media people who were eager to record the struggle and the changes for their viewers and readers. This was a mixed blessing. Gertrude Goldstein viewed the sudden avalanche of unsolicited publicity ambivalently; on the one hand, she was glad to see Woodward get favorable public exposure; on the other, it troubled her—and other staff members were resentful—that Woodward had suddenly become a *cause célèbre* over sex roles.

"After all," Gertrude commented, piqued, "this isn't the only good thing we've ever done." There is no doubt that having made its commitment to nonsexist education a matter of record through interviews with the New York *Times*, the *Wall Street Journal*, and several radio broadcasts, the school was obliged to follow through on its commitment with something that looked like unflagging zeal. The Sex-roles Committee felt happy, on the one hand, to be able to share their experiences with others who might be inspired to work for change at their own schools; and they felt, on the other hand, that the demands made on their time by outside groups (which were often glamorous, and therefore seductive) were taking them away from steady, sober, continuing earnest hard work at Woodward. There were also practical problems: how were we to decide with whom to speak, to whom to grant interviews (some people hate the New York *Times*, and other people hate the *Wall Street Journal* worse and regard accurate reportage in the Establishment press an impossibility)? Some people think that any vehicle is a good one if it reaches an audience we want to reach. How would we decide who would speak for the staff and for the committee? Decisions like these occasionally became rancorous because of lack of communication between the staff and the committee; several times the committee and the school administration accused each other of acting independently, without considering each other, out of a desire for power and notoriety. Gertrude says she thinks of that year as being "like the second year of a marriage"—the staff and the committee were committed to working together, but there were, in Gertrude's words, "post-honeymoon fights, fears, and misunderstandings." On one thing we were all agreed: the kinds of changes that had been wrought at Woodward were not of the kind that could be instantly translated into drama for television cameras. When major television networks asked to come into the school, we said no, not only to protect the children from the glaring intrusion, but also because the changes the staff and the Sex-roles Committee had brought about were too subtle to measure in this way.

How then had the school changed?

The curriculum, reading materials, the ways in which boys and girls relate to one another, work, play, and feel about themselves all reflect the raised consciousness of Woodward's staff.

Gertrude Goldstein says:

"I think even the most resistant staff member has moved. I think even if people are not ready to *be* different they're ready to *act* differently. I think they now see many instances of sexism where they didn't see it before."

Meg Bluhm, a third-and-fourth-grade teacher who acted as liaison between staff and committee says: "The staff became increasingly more positive toward the committee. At first the committee was perceived as a pressure group, trying to monopolize the staff's precious time. Now there is wide acceptance of the importance of the committee's goals. The present continuing dialogue among the staff about the relationships between men and women, and the relationships of adults with boys and with girls all started with the Sex-roles Committee. In the teachers' lunchroom, casual conversation reveals a much more positive feeling toward the committee, and excitement about programs and projected plans. There was some resentment of all the publicity the group got, but most people lay the blame for that on the media rather than on the committee."

Ruth Fishman says: "It's true some teachers do little about changing entrenched attitudes. Male teachers, particularly, still display some scorn, and more fear. They sit near one another at staff meetings—for comfort, I guess—and they probably feel outnumbered and overwhelmed. But we can't ever go back to being what we were before. There isn't anyone who isn't aware now. The curriculum has changed demonstrably. For example, I doubt that a year ago anyone would have thought of discussing the ACLU's women's rights litigation with a social studies class. This year, several teachers did. A year ago, seventh-grade girls would probably not have complained that boy-oriented problems in math books turned them off. Now they do complain. A third-grade teacher wrote to a textbook publisher to complain about a book called *Electricity for Young Boys*—and used the book-title as a consciousness-raising device for her third- and fourth-graders. The science classes reflect a new concern with whether sex-role behavior is instinctive or natural. There are small things too. Classroom illustrations have changed. You're not likely now to see a picture labeled '*woman* pioneer,' or '*female* farmer,' for example; and there are many more illustrations of black women and white women around than there used to be. Curriculum changes are less important than these subtle changes in attitudes and expectations."

An elective karate class was introduced (and half the takers were girls), the library devoted space to women's studies materials, the librarian began trying to combat ingrained and circumscribing attitudes of boys and girls toward book choices; and lower-grade teachers chose to read aloud more books in which girls were featured characters. Probably none of these changes was as significant as the change in the ways in which teachers began to encourage girls to extend themselves in previously neglected areas of activity.

The following anecdotes come from first-and-second- and third-and-fourth-grade teachers—Meg Bluhm, Trudie Lamb, and Bianca Posner:

"It used to be that when a girl complained she couldn't handle the saw at the woodworking bench, I'd call upon a competent child to help her, to make the activity less teacher-directed. Nine out of ten times, of course, the 'competent child' was a boy, who wanted to get to the bench anyway. Now I'm much more likely to get that girl to do it herself, even if it involves struggle. I tell her she doesn't have to do it all in one day. The idea is not that all girls have to be whizzes at woodworking, but that they learn not to lean on or be intimidated by the superior strength or ability of boys."

"I'm not even aware of all the things I do now, but I see the difference in the kids. Even the smallest girls now play kickball in outdoor games, the same ones that used to group together, and 'tell secrets,' and withdraw from physical activities. A lot of the girls wanted to play soccer, but were scared to compete with the boys. I started to play soccer with them, and that helped. Some of the boys made fun of the girls for being inept, and that scared them off again . . . I didn't treat that as a boy–girl thing; we just had long talks about how people related to others whose skills weren't as developed as theirs. I think it made the boys feel easier too, not to have to insist on their physical superiority."

"I'm conscious of not telling girls how pretty they look all the time; I find other things to reward them for, and now, when a girl chooses to read a story like *Cinderella*—which is really a sexist story when you think about it—I think it's important to question it—why did the Prince choose *her*?"

"At first, when my consciousness was raised, I used the words of the movement too much, was too explicit. I bludgeoned and came on too strong and turned the kids off. One day a girl said to me, 'That's the fourth time today you've said *Women's Lib.*' I did this for about a month after my initial involvement, and then I got smarter. I used to have to be sure the kids didn't miss the significance of anything, so I'd say, 'We've been reading lots of books about boys (we'd been studying pioneers—Davy Crockett, Kit Carsen, Johnny Appleseed), and none about girls. Now I'm going to read about a girl.' But the boys said, 'No, we're not.' So now I just do it, without talking about it. And the kids like it. They really pick up on things. I'm very conscious of sexist language, and when I read aloud I often make substitutions in pronouns. For instance, one day I read horse*person* for horse*man* (which I admit sounds funny), and Jennifer, who's eight, said, 'Come on, Meg, you know that book doesn't say *horseperson*.' We all laughed about it—but we discussed it, too."

"I never tried to stop boys from crying, I let them give their emotions full rein. But I realize now that I tended to squelch girls. I used to allow boys to fist-fight for a few minutes when there was a row, but I jumped in much faster with girls. I treat them the same way, now."

"The kids are much more aware of their own biases. The other day a boy said to me, 'Who's the man who discovered gravity . . . or the woman?' "

"I now assign chores like housekeeping, clean-up, messengering, mopping, straightening up, without regard to sex. I used to say, 'Is there a strong boy who'll help me carry chairs?' A seventh-grade girl pointed out to me that that was silly; she said, 'We're just as capable of carrying chairs as boys are. And you're not asking them because they're stronger. You're asking them, to make them *feel* stronger.' She was right of course."

"The best mathematician in my class is a girl. I admit I've been tempted to say, 'Myra's a girl, and she's good at math. Girls can be good at math.' But of course it's much better to say, 'Myra loves math and is good at it because she works at it.' That protects her from the jealousy of the kids who might reject her for being 'too good.' I think both boys and girls accept a boy's excelling much more easily than they do a girl's."

"I contrive situations to get what I want without resistance. In the lunchroom, girls had been sitting with girls and boys with boys. It was like enemy camps, with the boys making loud, snotty remarks about the girls, one of whom would usually end up in tears—or throw a piece of bread across the room. Nobody was really comfortable with it, but if I had assigned kids to tables, they'd have rebelled. What I did was to assign four waiters every day, two to a table, and the waiters were all girls, or all boys. So it meant there could never be a one-sex table. I didn't make a verbal point of it, but now it's happening naturally for boys and girls to sit together, and they enjoy it. It took me a long time to figure out how to do it. The real change is that girls and boys are beginning to relate to one another in a freer, more joyous way. There's a nice easy intermingling. It used to be possible to say, 'those are nice boys'; or, 'those are nice girls.' Now I can say, 'that's a nice *group*, a nice *class*.' Girls don't always group together now. That's good for them, and it's nice for the boys, too."

"Recently I read Lois Lensky's *Indian Captive*, a story about a pioneer girl who was captured by Indians and went to live in an Indian village. We talked about the difference in work habits, the different roles assigned to girls among the pioneers and among the Indians. Then the kids themselves took it into a discussion of how things were done in their own homes. Awareness breeds awareness; and the kids are very hip now. I heard this story about a girl in my class: she went to her doctor's office, and a little boy who was getting an injection was crying. The boy's father said, 'Boys have to be brave.' Jenny, the Woodward girl, said, 'I don't think boys have to be brave all the time, boys can cry.' The nurse humored her and said, 'That's right, honey, girls are really stronger, aren't they?' And Jenny said, 'No, girls aren't stronger; girls can cry and girls can be brave. Boys can cry and boys can be brave. It's what you feel like.' Jenny is seven."

Most teachers have become sensitive to the way language has been used to keep women conscious of their secondary, derivative roles. When, for example, a class visited the Museum of Natural History and saw the words *Evolution of Man* attached to an exhibit of a primitive woman nursing her baby, both teacher and children saw and commented on the ludicrousness of the designation.

When boys want to exclude girls from activities, teachers are now more likely to intervene: in a lower-grade class, children planned a play about astronauts. One girl did all the scenery and costumes, and the boys were glad to have her help. But when she wanted to perform, the boys protested: "Girls aren't astronauts." The teacher intervened, and the girl got the part. However, she felt obliged to announce, "I'm playing a boy now, because I'm an astronaut." The teacher used the occasion for a general discussion, appropriate to the situation, of sex-role stereotyping. Any one of a hundred anecdotes like this one might be offered as proof that Woodward is responding to the need for nonsexist education. But the most profound change is attitudinal: visitors to the school, when they are asked how it differs from others in its treatment of girls and boys usually remark on the awareness that seems to inform all the school's activities.

The translation of awareness into educational practice is difficult; there is no model to follow. Because there is no model to follow, and because old habits die hard, feminists feel that there are often lapses on the part of the staff, or opportunities missed: A notice sent to parents inviting them to curriculum workshops, for example, included a sketch of three boys all doing things—

holding up a banner, taking a picture, demonstrating woodworking tools. The one girl in the picture was doing nothing except to smile coyly and allow herself to be embraced by a protective boy. Sex-roles committeewomen were distressed. On another occasion, class lists were circulated with the Mr./Mrs. designation feminists abhor; some feminists reacted impatiently, with hot annoyance, eliciting this response from Gertrude Goldstein (who contended that the lists were the result of some bureaucratic bungle which was speedily adjusted): "People don't have a sense of proportion. Why isn't there more goodwill? Why can't people assume we're on the same side? Why do we have to keep proving it? Not every wish can be gratified; and communication isn't always easy. You have to see the whole picture. Don't act like little children who tell loving parents 'you don't love me' when one wish isn't gratified."

No position is pure; I sometimes wish it were possible for me to look upon sexism at Woodward with what a friend of mine calls "healing rage." But usually I am just confounded by the complexities and moral ambiguities that vitiate my own anger when something like this happens: I looked in, one day, on an eighth-grade class that had followed the trial of the Harlem Four; they had visited the courtroom, and talked with the defendants' lawyers, and now two of the Four were at Woodward, discussing their trial for murder and their long years in prison without bail, with eighth-graders and any other kids who chose to listen. Eighth-graders asked hard, sophisticated questions; a girl asked one of the Four, "Why do you think, if you were not at the scene of the murder, a fifteen-year-old girl told the police you were?" He responded, "She was just one of those bad kind of girls that you have to keep slapping around to keep them in their place." Aside from the fact that the question was serious enough not to have been shrugged off with a frivolous rejoinder, I was enraged at a reply that was so blatantly and cruelly sexist, angered that none of the kids called him on it, and furious with the teacher present who, in his zeal to demonstrate the evils of racism to the kids, allowed sexism to go unchallenged. On the other hand, I immediately mistrusted the intensity of my own reaction, and was unable, myself, to speak out for fear that whatever I said might be interpreted as racist—in fact I wondered if my reaction *was* racist. I saw that I was judging the militant blacks by their *macho* style, and I wondered if I were capable of dismissing real injustice because I did not find the victims of it attractive. I don't think there is any doubt that sensitive moral and political questions were raised by this incident. And we at Woodward are not yet at the place where we have established sufficient trust to be sure that all of the ramifications of incidents like these will be explored by feminists and staff, by teachers and older children, and by parents, black and white.

I asked Gertrude Goldstein how she saw the role of the Woodward feminists in the future:

"You have sown seeds that will flourish," she said. "Things will never be the same again. We ask you to continue to enrich our curriculum with books, films, and role models. What you bring us, we will utilize."

I asked several teachers what they thought the Sex-roles Committee should be doing:

"Don't disappear," they said. "Continue to work with the staff and with the children. Help us keep the issues alive. We need reminders until it's an integral part of all our attitudes. We need the continued support of parents. Changes take forever. Keep mobilizing. Each outside push helps the school along further."

And I asked several of the committee members:

"People are generally more accepting now that the basic ideas of the Movement have been legitimized. Maybe now we need to continue to raise our consciousness about behavioral issues, like, What does it do to a girl if you remove a doll or long dress from her? What about romance, and romantic love? We've made gains at Woodward, and established positions; maybe now it's time to consider the ramifications."

"We should be consultants. We can nudge. More important, we should tell the school, 'OK, get it together—we're available if you need us.' "

"We have to be watchdogs. We have to help the staff translate awareness into classroom action. I feel that we are now partners, rather than adversaries, in the lower school, but there is much work to be done with older kids. The emphasis should now be on

supplying curriculum and resource material rather than on raising consciousness. We have started the school on the road to
change."

"If we never appeared again, teachers with raised consciousness would raise the consciousness of others. In individual classrooms things would happen. Energy levels may die, but a new
wave of energetic feminists will come along."

But it does not look as if we are gone for good. The group
does, in fact, seem to have recaptured its early energy and zeal.
As I write this, in October 1972—less than one month into the
school year—black women and white women are arranging
meetings to discuss parent impact on the curriculum, and black
women are stimulating interest in taping oral histories. It is interesting and salutary, I think, that the impetus for these meetings
comes from the black women, who are saying that we must work
together for a nonsexist, nonracist curriculum at Woodward.
Each group—Black Studies and Sex Roles—has felt that it had
something to offer the school. I think we are beginning to see
that we have something to offer one another too. Consciousness-
raising meetings with teachers of older children are being ar-
ranged; new teachers who have come into the school have met
with Sex-roles Committee members, and lower-school teachers
have suggested discussion meetings to enable us all to translate
our awarenesses into classroom practice. Positive role models
have already been brought into the school and more visits are
planned. There is a sense of progress and renewal.


When the Sex-roles Committee at Woodward began to make its
influence felt at the school, the question we were asked most
frequently was, *What do you really want?* After a while, we
developed a certain facility in answering this once-onerous question (a facility that ignited into passion when we met with opposition or ill-will). It was easy, after all, to point to mechanical
changes we deemed necessary; easy, too, to say that we sought a
new awareness of sex-roles stereotyping. Our goals, thus defined,
were tangible, if not easily achieved. But in the course of two
years of consciousness-raising and political activity, we realized
that the question that underlay all our talk and all our action was

another, more difficult one. The question we were really asking ourselves and one another was, *Whom—what—do we want to be?*

What is true in the women's Movement in general is true for us at Woodward: it takes no great, bold imagining to say that women want equal pay for equal work, that they want the right to share in the work of the world and be rewarded appropriately, that they want control of their reproductive lives, that they want day-care centers; political, legal, and economic equality. But having said those things, and having committed ourselves to the struggle for them, we are left with more profound questions, which trouble and exercise our minds even as they exhilarate us, because we have never dared ask them before. When we talked and argued at Woodward about whether we valued more highly those characteristics traditionally associated with men or those traditionally associated with women; when we discussed whether our fulfillment meant aping men, we were not giving voice to bloodless abstractions: we were asking ourselves what we really wanted to be, and what we wanted our children to be. When we tried to define *work*, when we tried to define *success*, when we asked whether a person *is* what she *does*, we were asking ourselves to discover the source of our self-respect. We were also, as we sought to find a work in the world that would bring us joy, asking ourselves what we wanted the world to be. When we struggled with our attitudes toward the black women at Woodward, we were engaged in a visceral exploration of the meaning of that overused, underexamined, seductive word, *sisterhood*; and we were fighting to place our struggle in relation to the massive struggle against racism and class inequity. When, to understand emotional and intellectual realities, we argued, debated, cried, raged, fought, and sympathized, we were both living out the myths about women—that they are competitive with one another, that they are threatened by one another, that they are frightened of betrayal, that they are scared of a good fight, that they must always believe, or must always be, "nice"—and we were destroying the myths, as we sought a new, uncharted way to relate to one another, and to men. We were implicitly seeking a new definition of the supercharged words—aggression, hostility, compassion, judgment, kindness—that we have used to bludgeon ourselves into conformity or to cower from our real, fully articulated selves. We were asking ourselves how we *really* wished to behave, what our natures *really* demanded of us, what our ideal of social intercourse was, what we required from other people and of ourselves. Each of us was learning how to regard herself and other women as fully human beings. We were, in fact, asking ourselves—for our own sakes and for the sake of our children—*what it means to be fully human.* That, of course, is the central question that feminists must continue arduously and earnestly, to ask. The struggle for change at Woodward cannot basically be apprehended in terms of blocks and dolls and math and jump ropes; anymore than the women's Movement can be perceived as a quarrel about who does the dishes. What we are engaged in requires a comprehensive act of imagination: we are struggling to create ourselves, to understand our necessities, and to will our entailment in them. Our struggles to form a direct, purposeful connection with the world entail the obligation not only to contemplate and define our own singular individual natures and needs, but to understand the dynamics of oppression, so as to change the external realities that have the terrible power to invade and distort our inner reality, to make us less than fully human. Our desire to change ourselves is indistinguishable from our desire to change society, our desire to change the world.

Our work at Woodward is the good work—the unfinished work—of allowing all our children to become fully human.

True revolutionaries are like God—they create the world in their own image. Our awesome responsibility to ourselves, to our children, and to the future is to create ourselves in the image of goodness, because the future depends on the nobility of our imaginings.

# Bibliography

Altbach, Edith Hoshino, ed., *From Feminism to Liberation* (Cambridge, Mass.: Schenkman Publishing Co., 1971).

Bardwick, Judith M., *Psychology of Women: A Study of Biocultural Conflicts* (New York: Harper and Row, 1971; paperback edition, 1971, Harper and Row).

de Beauvoir, Simone, *Second Sex* (New York: Alfred A. Knopf, Inc., 1953; paperback edition, Bantam Books).

Bernard, Jessie, *The Future of Marriage* (New York: World Publishing Co., 1971).

Bird, Carolin, *Born Female* (New York: David McKay Company, Inc., 1970; paperback edition, 1971, Pocket Books).

Cade, Toni, ed., *Black Woman: An Anthology* (New York: New American Library, Signet paperback, 1970).

Davis, Elizabeth Gould, *The First Sex* (New York: G. P. Putnam's Sons, 1971).

Drake, Kirsten, Marks, Dorothy, and Wexford, Mary, *Women's Work and Women's Studies, 1971: An Interdisciplinary Bibliography* (New York: Barnard Women's Center, 1972; available from KNOW, Inc., P.O. Box 86031, Pittsburgh, Pennsylvania 15221).

Firestone, Shulamith, *Dialectic of Sex: The Case for Feminist Revolution* (William Morrow & Company, Inc., 1970).

Flexner, Eleanor, *Century of Struggle: The Women's Rights Movement in the U.S.* (New York: Atheneum Publishers, 1959).

Flynn, Elizabeth Gurley, *I Speak My Own Price* (Boston: Masses and Mainstream, 1955).

Friedan, Betty, *Feminine Mystique,* (New York: W. W. Norton & Company, Inc., 1963; paperback edition, Dell Books).

Gilman, Charlotte Perkins, *Women and Economics: The Economic Factor between Men and Women As a Factor in Social Evolution*, Carl N. Degler, ed., (New York: Harper and Row, Torch Books, 1970).

Gornick, Vivian and Moran, Barbara, eds., *Woman in Sexist Society* (New York: New American Library, Signet paperback, 1972).

Greer, Germaine G., *The Female Eunuch* (New York: Bantam Books, 1972).

Heilbrun, Carolyn G., *Toward a Recognition of Androgyny* (New York: Alfred A. Knopf, 1973).

James, Edward T., ed.; James, Janet Wilson and Boyer, Paul S., asst. eds., *Notable American Women 1607–1950: A Biographical Dictionary* (Boston: Harvard University Press, Belknap Press, 1972).

Janeway, Elizabeth, *Man's World, Woman's Place: A Study in Social Mythology* (William Morrow & Company, Inc., 1972; paperback edition, Dell Books, 1972).

Jones, Mother, *The Autobiography of Mother Jones*, Mary F. Parton, ed., (C. H. Kerr, 1972).

Lerner, Gerda, *Black Women in White America* (New York: Pantheon Books, Inc., 1972).

Lerner, Gerda, *Grimké Sisters from South Carolina: Pioneers for Women's Rights and Abolition (Studies in the Life of Women)* (New York: Schocken Books, Inc., 1971).

Merriam, Eve, *Double Bed* (New York: M. Evans & Company, Inc., 1972).

Millett, Kate, *Sexual Politics* (New York: Doubleday Publishing Company, 1970; paperback edition, Avon Books, 1971).

Mitchell, Juliet, *Woman's Estate* (New York: Pantheon Books, Inc., 1972).

Morgan, Elaine, *The Descent of Woman* (New York: Stein & Day Publishers, 1972).

Morgan, Robin, ed., *Sisterhood is Powerful: An Anthology of Writings from the Women's Liberation Movement* (New York: Random House, Inc., 1970).

Rowbotham, Sheila, *Women, Resistance and Revolution: A History of Women & Revolution in the Modern World* (New York: Pantheon Books, Inc., 1972).

Schneir, Miriam, ed., *Feminism* (New York: Random House, Inc., 1971; paperback edition, Vintage Books).

Seaman, Barbara, *Free and Female: The Sex Life of the Contemporary Woman* (New York: Coward McCann & Geoghegan, Inc., 1972).

Showalter, Elaine, *Women's Liberation & Literature* (New York: Harcourt, Brace Jovanovich, Inc., 1971).

Tanner, Leslie B., ed., *Voices from Women's Liberation* (New York: New American Library, Signet paperback, 1971).

Theodore, Athena, ed., *Professional Woman* (New York: Schenkman Publishing Company, 1971).

Thompson, Mary, ed., *Voices of the New Feminism* (New York: Beacon Press, 1970).

Wollstonecraft, Mary, *Vindication of the Rights of Women*, Charles W. Hagelman, Jr., ed. (New York: Norton Library, 1967).

Woolf, Virginia, *A Room of One's Own* (New York: Harcourt, Brace Jovanovich, Inc., 1929).